ENDORSEMENTS

I have known Chazdon for only a few years in the natural, but from the moment we met, there was an instant recognition in the Spirit—a kindred connection in the glory realm. As we talked, he shared how our ministry had impacted him through the books we've written and the soaking music we've released. That conversation reminded me of a powerful spiritual truth: impartation is real. When we open our hearts to receive—whether through sitting under an anointed ministry, reading a Spirit-breathed book, or listening to worship that carries God's presence—the grace and revelation resting on another life can flow into our own. This book carries that kind of impartation.

While sitting under Chazdon's ministry last fall, I could sense the grace of God's glory resting upon him. Not just through the words he spoke, but through the atmosphere that surrounded those words. One line in this book especially stirred my heart: "The world does not need more arguments about God's existence; it needs evidence of His reality." That statement captures the cry of this generation and the message of this book. When believers carry the glory of God, His reality becomes undeniable. It takes glory to produce glory, and Chazdon has clearly spent time in the presence of Jesus. From that place of encounter, he now ministers with authority and clarity. I believe this book will unlock a supernatural dimension for those who are hungry to receive from God. I have been blessed by his ministry, and I know you will be too.

Joshua Mills
Bestselling author, *Moving in Glory Realms*
Founder, International Glory Ministries
Palm Springs, CA
www.JoshuaMills.com

We are living in days of extraordinary miracles. In *Unlocking Heaven's Power*, Chazdon Strickland helps unlock the supernatural power of God so you can experience the miraculous in your life.

Sid Roth
Host, *It's Supernatural!*

Chazdon Strickland is a practitioner of the supernatural, and I believe this timely book will provoke and ignite you to do the same. Not only has he done his biblical homework, but Chazdon is a bold risk-taker who is pressing in to see "book of Acts" Christianity as the reality in his life today. And the good news is you can do the same thing! Let this book be like a mentoring masterclass, not from someone who claims superiority, but from a man who has never stopped being hungry for Jesus, and who wants to see every believer unlock God's supernatural in their lives.

Larry Sparks, MDiv.
Sparks Ministries
Bestselling author of *Pentecostal Fire*
Vice President of Publishing, Nori Media Group

In a generation hungry for authentic power and desperate for a true demonstration of the Spirit, Chazdon Strickland delivers a master key. *Unlocking Heaven's Power* is not merely a book to be read; it is a mantle to be worn and a weapon to be wielded.

Chazdon brilliantly dismantles the religious paradigms that have kept the Church in bondage and systematically guides you into the reality of your God-given identity. This book is a divine summons to move beyond theory and into tangible, supernatural outcomes. Each chapter is a strategic download, equipping you to confront darkness, break every resistance, and partner with Heaven's agenda for your life.

I felt the anointing leap from every page. This is a timely, prophetic mandate for every believer who is tired of empty words and is ready to walk in undeniable power. Read it, apply it, and prepare to become the sign and wonder you were created to be.

Charlie Shamp
Prophet and Author
Destiny Encounters International
Renaissance Coalition

Chazdon Strickland is a pioneer in the supernatural. With his practical approach to signs and wonders, Chazdon has equipped thousands of people to operate in the power of the Holy Spirit.

In his brand-new book *Unlocking Heaven's Power*, Apostle Chazdon leads the reader on a journey of discovering their divine inheritance in Christ: a supernatural lifestyle. As you read, you will learn how to confront fear, doubt, and religious limitations and release the power of the Spirit in every area of your life.

Dr. Kynan Bridges
Apostolic Leader, Pastor, and Bestselling Author

Unlocking Heaven's Power

Destiny Image Books by Chazdon Strickland

Out by Fire: Receiving Deliverance and Expelling Demons through the Power, Presence and Glory of God

Supernatural Upgrade: Keys to Walking in the Glory Realm

UNLOCKING HEAVEN'S POWER

Activating Your God-Given Authority to
Confront Darkness, Break Resistance, and
Release Supernatural Outcomes

CHAZDON STRICKLAND

 All emphasis within Scripture quotations is the author's own. Take note that the name satan and related names are not capitalized. We choose not to acknowledge him, even to the point of violating grammatical rules.

DESTINY IMAGE® PUBLISHERS, INC.
P.O. Box 310, Shippensburg, PA 17257-0310
"Publishing cutting-edge prophetic resources to supernaturally empower the body of Christ"

This book and all other Destiny Image and Destiny Image Fiction books are available at Christian bookstores and distributors worldwide.

For more information on foreign distributors, call 717-532-3040.
Reach us on the Internet: www.destinyimage.com.

ISBN 13 TP: 979-8-8815-0807-4
ISBN 13 eBook: 979-8-8815-0808-1

For Worldwide Distribution, Printed in the U.S.A.
1 2 3 4 5 6 7 8 / 30 29 28 27 26

CONTENTS

FOREWORD

In the pages of this book, you will find more than words—you will encounter a living revelation of the Word and the Spirit. These truths are not merely to be read, but to be received, embraced, and walked out in your daily life. As you journey through each chapter, you will begin to see with greater clarity the power of God, the depth of your intimate knowledge, and the authority that has been entrusted to you as a believer.

This book is an invitation—an invitation to step beyond surface-level understanding and into the deep, transformative ways and wisdom of God. It calls you to awaken to your divine purpose and to walk in the same power and demonstration that marked the life and ministry of Jesus Christ. The works of Christ were never meant to be admired from a distance; they were meant to be continued through yielded vessels who understand their identity, intimacy, and authority in Him.

As you read, expect the Holy Spirit to illuminate the Scriptures in fresh and profound ways. Expect to encounter the power of God in a way that is not distant or theoretical, but active and present in your life. Expect your relationship with Jesus to deepen into a place of true intimacy—where you not only know about Him, but truly know Him. And expect your understanding of spiritual authority to expand, empowering you to walk boldly in what has already been given to you.

There is an impartation within these pages—a stirring that will draw you into deeper fellowship with Christ and a greater awareness of His power at work within you. Limitations will be challenged, faith will be stretched, and you will begin to move with a new confidence in the authority that flows from your union with Him.

Prepare yourself to be transformed. Prepare to see differently, think differently, and believe differently. This is not just a journey of knowledge, but of encounter. As your understanding expands, so will your capacity to carry and release the power of God in every sphere of your life.

Prepare to be increased in your intimate knowledge of Jesus—His power, His presence, and the authority you carry in His name. The heavens are not distant; they are accessible. And through the revelation contained in this book, you are being positioned to walk in the fullness of what has already been made available to you.

Step in with expectation. Receive with openness. And walk forward in the power of heaven.

Apostle Tony Kemp
President, Tony Kemp Ministries
The Acts Group

INTRODUCTION

BEYOND WORDS—THE RETURN OF DIVINE DEMONSTRATION

There are moments in history when words alone are no longer enough. There are seasons when explanations fail, and even the most accurate theology alone does not awaken a sleeping generation. In those moments, heaven does not respond with more discussion—it responds with demonstration. God has always reserved the right to interrupt human doubt, complacency, and compromise with unmistakable displays of His power. Yet from Genesis to Revelation, those displays have never existed for their own sake. Every sign, every wonder, and every miracle has always served a greater purpose: to reveal who God is and to point hearts back to Him.

In the days of Elijah, Israel was not suffering from a lack of information about God; they were suffering from a lack of demonstration. They knew the stories of deliverance. They carried the law. They could recount the acts of God performed for their ancestors. Yet despite this knowledge, their hearts were divided, their worship was compromised, and their faith had grown passive. Altars lay broken, covenant became cultural, and truth was reduced to theory rather than transformation. The crisis of that hour was not atheism, but a mixture of beliefs. Israel had not rejected God outright; they had attempted to add other allegiances, other voices, and other sources of power alongside Him. Baal worship coexisted with Yahweh worship, and the people believed they could live in the tension of divided loyalty without consequence.

It was into that confusion that Elijah stepped—not as a philosopher, not as a negotiator, but as a man carrying authority. The turning point did not come through persuasion, tradition, or compromise. It came when fire fell. Heaven responded. The living God revealed Himself through undeniable power. That fire was more than a miracle; it was a verdict. It settled the question of who was truly God. It restored clarity to a confused people and called a nation back to covenant, not through pressure, but through power. The miracle did not terminate in amazement—it terminated in revelation. The fire pointed beyond itself and forced the people to declare, "*The Lord, He is God*" (1 Kings 18:39 NKJV).

Our generation stands in a strikingly similar moment. We live in an age saturated with sermons, content, podcasts, conferences, books, and conversations about God, yet marked by confusion, compromise, and spiritual fatigue. Never before has the Church had access to so much information, and never before has there been such a visible disconnect between what is preached and what is experienced. Many know about God, but few expect Him to act. Faith has been reduced to philosophy—authority has been replaced with apology, and conviction has been softened into comfort. In some corners of the Church, the supernatural has been quietly relegated to the past—honored in Scripture but dismissed in experience. God's power is acknowledged in theory while avoided in practice. Miracles are celebrated in stories from somewhere else, some other time, but rarely expected here and now.

There is a growing belief, spoken or unspoken, that God's power was for then, not now; that miracles were for the early Church but not the modern one; that signs and wonders were necessary in biblical times but unnecessary, unreliable, or even dangerous today. In an attempt to appear reasonable, sophisticated, or safe, many have settled for a faith that explains away what God never withdrew. Some have redefined faith as little more than personal morality. Others have reduced Christianity to social good. Still others have replaced spiritual authority with endless caution. The tragic result is a Church often rich in language but poor in evidence—and in the absence of evidence, the revelation of Jesus becomes blurred rather than magnified.

Yet heaven has not changed its mind. The same God who answered by fire still answers today. The same Spirit who empowered prophets, apostles, and ordinary believers has not gone silent. The same authority Jesus delegated to His followers has not expired, and the same commission to heal the sick, cast out demons, proclaim the Kingdom, and demonstrate God's power remains fully intact. But the purpose remains unchanged as well: signs are never meant to glorify the vessel, elevate the experience, or replace the message. They exist to confirm the Word and to reveal Jesus as Lord. The problem is not a lack of power; it is a lack of access, understanding, and bold authority to release what has already been given—always in a way that leads people to Christ.

This book is an invitation to return to that place of holy expectation. *Unlocking Heaven's Power* is not about hype or emotionalism. It is not about manufacturing moments, chasing experiences, or elevating spectacle above substance. It is about alignment—rediscovering the authority Jesus entrusted to believers and learning how to walk in agreement with heaven so that God's will is not only prayed, but manifested. It is about moving from passive belief to active faith, from hoping for a breakthrough to releasing it, from admiring miracles to becoming conduits of them—while never losing sight of the truth that every miracle is meant to testify to Jesus.

Just as in Elijah's day, the world does not need more arguments about God's existence; it needs evidence of His reality. It needs a Church unafraid to believe that what God promised, He still performs. Yet it also needs a Church anchored in the understanding that the power of God does not exist to entertain curiosity, but to awaken hearts to the knowledge of Him. The question then—and now—is the same: if God is truly God, will we allow Him to answer by fire in a way that turns hearts back to Him?

Recently, I was invited to travel to Israel with a close friend, a journey that would mark me far more deeply than I expected. Among the many sacred and historic locations we visited, one site in particular arrested my spirit—Mount Carmel. In this very place, Elijah confronted the false prophets, where fire fell, and where heaven spoke. Though I had read, studied, preached, and taught this story countless times, standing there in person brought an entirely new weight and clarity to the Scriptures. The Bible was no longer a distant record of ancient events; it was alive beneath my feet.

As we stood on Mount Carmel, our tour guide explained something I had never heard before. In Jewish tradition, the fire that fell from heaven upon Elijah's altar is referred to simply as "the miracle of fire." Not because it was one miracle among many, but because it was the miracle—an unmistakable, defining moment in Israel's history. Then came a detail that shifted my understanding forever. The guide explained that when the fire fell, it was visible far beyond the immediate gathering. From Mount Carmel's elevated position, the surrounding regions and even neighboring nations would have seen it. This was not a small, contained flame quietly consuming an altar. It was a divine announcement, a public declaration, a supernatural event designed not merely to convince those present, but to broadcast a message to the world: Jehovah is God.

In all my years of studying this account recorded in Scripture, I had never fully considered the scale of that moment. I had imagined fire falling upon an altar. Still, not fire falling in such a way that entire regions could witness it, not fire functioning as a signpost for nations, not fire powerful enough to turn hearts by its sheer undeniability. Standing there, something awakened in me. I realized that when heaven's power is unlocked, it is never meant to remain small, private, or contained. God's power is not designed merely for personal encouragement; it is designed for public transformation—and ultimately for public revelation. When heaven moves, families turn, communities shift, cities awaken, and even nations are impacted, not because fire fell, but because hearts are confronted with the reality of God.

This is what takes place when we unlock heaven's power. Elijah's miracle did more than prove God's existence; it restored covenant identity, dismantled false authority, exposed counterfeit power, and demanded a response. No one walked away neutral, and no one remained undecided. The fire forced clarity, but the clarity pointed to God Himself. Our generation desperately needs that kind of clarity again. We live in a world overwhelmed by competing voices, spiritual confusion, and diluted truth. People are not merely asking whether God exists; they are asking whether He intervenes, whether He heals, whether He speaks, whether He delivers, and whether He still transforms lives in real time. A powerless gospel cannot answer those questions, but neither can a power divorced from revelation. A demonstrated Kingdom that points unmistakably to Jesus can.

This is the hour in which our understanding of spiritual authority is awakening. God is once again stirring hearts to believe that the Christian life was never meant to be merely endured—it was meant to be empowered. The Holy Spirit is not an accessory to faith; He is the engine. The Kingdom of God is not a concept; it is a reality meant to be revealed through God's people, always in a way that reflects the nature and character of Christ. This book exists to stir the miracle workers and the demonstrators of the Spirit's power in our time, not to draw attention to themselves, but to bear witness to Jesus.

In fact, this book is not only for those who desire to operate in signs and wonders, but for those God is raising to become signs and wonders—men and women whose lives so clearly reflect heaven's authority that their very presence points others to Christ, whose obedience invites divine interruption, whose faith creates space for miracles, and whose lives serve as living evidence that Jesus is alive, reigning, and active today. A life filled with God's power is possible. Victorious outcomes are possible. Supernatural breakthroughs are possible—not for a select few or spiritual elites, but for believers willing to understand their authority, align with heaven, and walk in bold faith with Jesus at the center.

It is time to unlock heaven's power—not so we can be impressive, but so God can be unmistakable; not so we can be exalted, but so Jesus can be revealed; not so we can chase fire, but so fire can once again fall and point hearts back to Him. The altar is ready, heaven is willing, and the only question that remains is this: will we dare to believe that God still answers by fire—and that when He does, it is always for His glory and for the revelation of Jesus Christ?

CHAPTER 1
RESTORING YOUR DOMINION AND AUTHORITY

And Jesus came and spake unto them, saying, all power is given unto me in heaven and in earth
(Matthew 28:18 KJV).

I can only imagine how mystifying it must have been for those who were about to be born into the early Church to realize that Christ had truly been raised from the dead. The resurrection was not merely something they believed; it was a reality they witnessed. Scripture tells us that Jesus showed Himself alive by many infallible proofs, and I imagine the atmosphere around Him carried a raw, tangible glory as He appeared to them in His resurrected body. No doubt their hearts were filled with awe, wonder, and questions. What had the cross accomplished? What had the resurrection changed? What did this mean for the world and for them? The truth is, everything had changed—permanently—both in the spiritual realm and in the natural realm.

To understand what changed, we must carefully consider what Jesus declared just before He ascended. Standing before

His disciples not as the suffering servant but as the risen Lord, Jesus made this extraordinary announcement: *"All power is given unto me in heaven and in earth."* This was not poetic language or symbolic encouragement; it was a legal and authoritative declaration. In this statement are two truths that demand our attention. First, Jesus said all power had been given to Him. Second, He identified the scope of that power by naming two realms—heaven and earth. Both were intentional, and both reveal what the cross and resurrection truly accomplished. The word translated power in this verse is the Greek word *exousia*, which means authority, legal permission, the right to rule and act, and sovereign jurisdiction. Jesus was not saying He had received a new miraculous ability. Throughout His earthly ministry, He had already healed the sick, raised the dead, multiplied food, walked on water, cast out demons, and demonstrated supernatural power in countless ways. What He received after the resurrection was not the ability to perform miracles, but the absolute authority to rule. And He did not receive some authority—He received all authority. This authority was complete, final, and uncontested.

After the fall of man, the authority God had given Adam was forfeited through disobedience. Adam had been entrusted with dominion over the earth under God's authority, but through sin, that dominion was surrendered. As a result, everything under Adam's jurisdiction became subject to satan's influence, which is why Scripture refers to him as the god of this world. Satan did not receive authority over the earth by divine assignment; he usurped it through deception. When satan and the rebellious angels fell, they were not given the earth; they took advantage of humanity's fall. From Adam's disobedience until the resurrection of Jesus, authority on the earth was contested territory.

When Jesus made this declaration, He was announcing that the contest was over. Dominion had been legally restored. What had been lost through Adam had now been recovered through obedience. What had been disputed since the fall could no longer be disputed. By declaring that all authority existed in both heaven and earth, Jesus made it clear that no realm remained outside His jurisdiction. Authority in the spiritual realm and authority in the natural realm were now unified under His lordship. Nothing remained unresolved, and nothing remained contested.

This declaration was not made for Jesus' benefit alone; it was made to establish the foundation for everything that would follow. The Great Commission flows directly from this moment. The Church would not advance by human strength or persuasion, but by delegated authority rooted in Christ's victory. From this point forward, all signs, wonders, miracles, and victories would operate under one governing reality: Jesus Christ reigns. Every demonstration of power exists for one ultimate purpose—to point hearts back to Him. One of the great misunderstandings in the Church today is that many believers still view the devil through the lens of his pre-resurrection authority. Often, preachers unintentionally magnify satan's influence while simultaneously minimizing the Church's position. In doing so, the enemy is portrayed as overwhelmingly powerful, while believers are left seeing themselves as weak, defensive, and barely surviving. This imbalance does not come from Scripture; it comes from failing to fully understand what was accomplished through the cross and resurrection.

When Jesus conquered death, descended into the realm of the dead, and rose victorious, satan lost the keys of death and hell. His kingdom was not merely challenged—it was disarmed. Scripture tells us that through His death, Jesus spoiled principalities and powers, openly triumphing over them. This means satan was stripped of legal authority. His claim was revoked. His jurisdiction was dismantled. He was exposed as an illegitimate ruler operating without lawful standing. This does not mean that satan ceased to exist, nor that darkness has no activity in the world. It means satan no longer possesses authority. He may still have influence, deception, and ability, but he no longer has the right to rule. He operates as a defeated adversary, not a reigning king. His power exists only where his lies are believed and where his illegitimacy goes unchallenged.

The resurrection of Jesus did not merely mark His victory over death; it established a new position for redeemed humanity. Scripture tells us that when God raised Christ from the dead, He did more than vindicate His Son—He inaugurated a new order. Jesus was seated at the right hand of the Father, far above all principality, power, might, and dominion. Yet the astonishing claim of the New Testament is that believers are not only beneficiaries of this exaltation—they are participants in it. Paul writes that God "*...raised us up together, and made us sit together in heavenly places in Christ Jesus...*" (Ephesians 2:6 NKJV). This language is deliberate and unmistakable. To be seated with Christ is not only a future promise; it is a present spiritual reality. Seating speaks of rest, rule, and authority. Kings sit. Rulers sit. Those who have completed their work sit. The posture of seating indicates that victory has already been secured and that authority is now exercised from a position of completion rather than striving.

This does not mean believers are exalted independently of Christ. Rather, they are exalted in Him. Union with Christ is the central reality of salvation. Everything Jesus accomplished—His obedience, death, resurrection, ascension, and enthronement—becomes accessible to believers through union, not imitation. We do not attempt to climb into authority; we are placed into it by grace. This is why Paul repeatedly uses phrases such as *in Christ, with Christ,* and *through Christ.* Authority flows from relationship, not effort. Being seated with Christ means believers now live from a heavenly position while still operating on the earth. This is not escapism or detachment from reality; it is governmental alignment. From this seated position, believers do not fight for victory—they enforce what Christ has already accomplished. Spiritual warfare, prayer, and ministry are not desperate attempts to convince God to act; they are expressions of agreement with what heaven has already established.

This seated reality connects directly to Scripture's declaration that believers are made kings and priests unto God. The language of kingship and priesthood is deeply rooted in God's original design for humanity. In the beginning, Adam was created to function as both ruler and steward—governing the earth under God's authority while maintaining communion with Him. Sin fractured this design, separating rulership from relationship. Kings ruled without holiness, and priests ministered without authority. In Christ, the two are reunited. Jesus fulfills both offices perfectly. He is the King who reigns with righteousness and the High Priest who intercedes eternally. Through union with Him, believers are restored to this dual calling. As kings, they exercise authority under Christ's lordship. As priests, they maintain access, intimacy, and mediation through worship and prayer. Kingship without priesthood becomes tyranny; priesthood without kingship becomes powerlessness. In Christ, believers carry both kingship and priesthood—authority grounded in intimacy.

This kingship is not political domination or self-exaltation. It is delegated authority expressed through obedience. Kings under Christ rule by enforcing His will, not their own. They do not create law; they administer what has already been decreed. This is why Jesus taught His disciples to pray, *"Your kingdom come. Your will be done on earth as it is in heaven"* (Matthew 6:10 NKJV). Kingship is exercised through alignment, not independence. Priesthood, likewise, is not merely a ritual—it is access. Through salvation, believers are granted continual access to God's presence. The veil that once separated humanity from God has been torn permanently. This access is not earned through discipline or maturity; it is granted through Christ's finished work. From this place of access, believers minister unto the Lord and represent heaven to the earth.

This restored identity is made possible because believers partake of the divine nature. Scripture says that through God's promises, believers become partakers of His divine nature, having escaped the corruption that is in the world through lust. The Greek word for *partakers* implies participation or sharing, not ownership. Believers do not become divine in essence, but they do share in God's life through regeneration. At salvation, the human spirit is recreated. This is not metaphorical—it is a spiritual reality. The spirit that was once dead is made alive by the Spirit of God. This is why Jesus referred to salvation as being born from above. The believer now carries the life of God within, not merely as influence, but as an indwelling presence. The Holy Spirit does not visit; He abides.

This participation in the divine nature restores access to the spirit realm. Prior to salvation, humanity is spiritually disconnected, governed primarily by the natural senses. After salvation, the believer becomes spiritually alive and capable of perceiving, responding to, and operating from the realm of the Spirit. This does not eliminate natural reasoning; it brings it under spiritual governance. Jesus modeled this life perfectly. He lived fully in the natural world while remaining continuously aligned with the Father. He did not react to circumstances; He responded from communion. His authority flowed from intimacy. After His resurrection, He invited believers into this same pattern of life—not as gods, but as sons and daughters united to the Son.

Being seated with Christ, reigning as kings and priests, and partaking of the divine nature are not separate truths—they are one reality viewed from different angles. Seating speaks of position. Kingship speaks of authority. Priesthood speaks of access. Divine nature speaks of capacity. Together, they describe the restored life of the believer in Christ. Yet all of this must remain anchored in humility. Authority does not exist to elevate the believer; it exists to reveal Jesus. Kingship is exercised in service. Priesthood is expressed in surrender. Participation in the divine nature produces holiness, not arrogance. The closer believers walk in authority, the more clearly Christ should be seen.

The ultimate goal of this restored position is not power for its own sake, but representation. Believers are seated so they can reign, reign so they can serve, and serve so Christ can be revealed. Heaven's authority is released on earth through those who know who they are in Him. Jesus reigns now, seated at the right hand of the Father, and astonishingly, those who are in Him reign with Him—not as rivals, but as redeemed sons and daughters carrying His authority, reflecting His nature, and advancing His Kingdom until the day He is revealed in fullness.

Because we are seated with Christ, share in His authority, and partake of His divine nature, the implications are unavoidable. If our position in Him is real and present, then the life that flows from that position must also be real and present. If Jesus truly passed authority to the Church, then it becomes impossible to argue that the supernatural is no longer for today. You cannot separate authority from function, nor can you separate the Holy Spirit from manifestation. To do so is to misunderstand both the nature of the Spirit and the intent of Christ's commission. Jesus did not declare that all authority belonged to Him simply to make a theological point; He declared it so that He could delegate it. The Great Commission is not a suggestion; it is an authorized sending. Christ's authority did not terminate in heaven—it was released through His body on the earth. If that authority is still intact, as Scripture makes clear, then the expression of that authority must also still be intact. Otherwise, authority becomes theoretical rather than functional, and the commission becomes symbolic rather than actionable.

The supernatural is not an optional feature of Christianity; it is the natural outworking of a supernatural Kingdom. Jesus did not instruct His disciples to talk about the Kingdom merely—He instructed them to demonstrate it. He did not say the Kingdom was coming someday; He said it was at hand. The evidence of that Kingdom was not found in words alone, but in power. If the authority Jesus carried was necessary to demonstrate the Kingdom, then why would that same authority be unnecessary now? The idea that the supernatural ceased is not rooted in Scripture; it is rooted in experience—or rather, the lack of it. When expectation diminishes, theology often adjusts to protect disappointment. But Scripture never teaches that the authority of Christ would outlast the expression of His power. In fact, the opposite is true. Jesus said that the works He did would continue and even increase in reach because He was going to the Father. His ascension did not mark the end of power; it marked its multiplication.

This brings us to a question that must be asked honestly: how can the Holy Spirit live in a believer and that believer be no different from someone who does not have the Spirit? If the same Spirit who raised Jesus from the dead now dwells in us, then something must be different—not hypothetically, but tangibly. The indwelling Spirit is not symbolic, dormant, or passive. He is active, alive, and powerful.

Salvation does not merely change a destination; it changes a nature. The believer is recreated, indwelt, and empowered. The Holy Spirit does not take up residence in us simply to make us morally improved versions of our former selves. He comes to restore communion, reveal Christ, and release heaven's life through us. To claim that the Spirit lives within, yet produces no spiritual fruit, no authority, no witness, and no power, is to reduce Him to an abstract concept rather than a living Person.

The early Church did not wrestle with whether the supernatural was for them—they assumed it, expected it, and operated in it because they understood authority. When persecution came, they did not pray for safety; they prayed for boldness and power. When sickness appeared, they did not defer to explanation; they enforced the name of Jesus. When demons manifested, they did not negotiate; they commanded. None of this was driven by spiritual elitism but by spiritual understanding. What has changed is not heaven's posture, but the Church's expectation.

If the Holy Spirit still convicts, regenerates, sanctifies, and reveals Christ, then He must also still empower. The Spirit cannot be divided against Himself. You cannot affirm His presence while denying His expression. The same Spirit who inspired the Word is the Spirit who confirms the Word. Signs and wonders were never meant to replace faith; they were meant to support it. They were never the message; they were the evidence that the message was true.

The fear surrounding the supernatural often comes from misuse, not from truth. Abuse does not negate proper use. Counterfeit does not eliminate the genuine. Jesus never withdrew authority because some would mishandle it—He entrusted it anyway, knowing that relationship, not fear, was the safeguard. If believers today look no different than the world in power, authority, peace, or spiritual impact, the answer is not to redefine Christianity but to rediscover it. The solution is not to explain away power, but to return to intimacy, alignment, and obedience. Authority flows best through surrender. Power flows best through humility. The Spirit moves most freely where Jesus remains the center.

The passing of authority from Jesus to the Church did not diminish His reign—it extended it. He reigns in heaven and expresses that reign through His body on the earth. To deny the supernatural today is not humility; it is contradiction. If Christ reigns and His Spirit lives in us, then heaven must still touch earth. Anything less would suggest that resurrection power stops at salvation, and Scripture makes it clear that it does not. The Holy Spirit in you was never meant to be hidden; He was given so that the life of Jesus could be seen, known, and experienced today.

A striking illustration of what it looks like to exercise authority, not merely discuss it, is found in a well-known testimony about a confrontation between the Kingdom of God and organized spiritual darkness in Nigeria. At a time when occult practices were being spoken of openly and without shame, an international witchcraft convention was reportedly announced. The gathering was intended to bring together practitioners from various regions and nations—an audacious declaration that spiritual darkness believed it could operate publicly and without resistance. What made the moment especially sobering was not only the announcement itself, but the confidence behind it. One of the organizers appeared publicly and made a chilling boast when questioned about divine intervention: "Even if God were to come down Himself, He could not stop this meeting." The statement was more than blasphemous; it revealed a spiritual assumption that heaven was distant and disengaged, and that no authority existed on the earth capable of resisting what had been planned.

Soon after, the confrontation moved into full public view when both a Christian pastor and a representative connected to the event appeared on national television. The exchange was no longer hidden or theoretical; it was visible to an entire nation. On air, the same claim was repeated, expressing confidence that God was enthroned in heaven but irrelevant on earth, and that the Church held no enforceable authority. Many believers watching responded with fear or silence. It is one thing to affirm Christ's victory in doctrine; it is another to believe that His victory must be enforced in real time, in real places, and under public scrutiny.

The apostle, however, interpreted the moment through a different lens. He understood something foundational: authority does not originate in heaven's activity alone; it is exercised through heaven's representatives on earth. Rather than appealing to political systems, organizing protests, or calling for demonstrations, he committed himself to prayer and fasting. He immersed himself in Scripture not to persuade God to act, but to align himself with what God had already accomplished through Christ. His confidence rested on the conviction that Jesus had already defeated the powers of darkness and that believers were commissioned to stand in that victory.

On national television, he responded directly to the boast that had been made and reportedly declared that the convention would not be held. He added words that revealed his understanding of delegated authority with unmistakable clarity: "God will not have to come down from His throne to stop this meeting. He has already sent me here." This was not arrogance but representation. He was not claiming independent power or equality with God; he was asserting the principle that heaven governs the earth through those who are seated with Christ and sent in His name. God's power was not diminished by remaining enthroned—it was expressed through obedience on earth.

According to the testimony that followed, the convention unraveled. Plans collapsed, confusion overtook the organizers, and the gathering never reached its intended conclusion. Whether one approaches this account as a historical record or as a faith testimony, the theological lesson remains clear: darkness does not retreat because God descends; it retreats because authority is exercised by those who understand their commission. This story is not about spectacle or spiritual theatrics. It is a reminder that authority in Christ is not passive. Jesus did not say that all authority might be given to Him—He said it has been given, and having received it, He delegated it.

The tragedy of the modern Church is not a lack of power, but a misunderstanding of responsibility. We often ask God to intervene where He has already authorized us to stand. We pray for movement in heaven when heaven is waiting for obedience on earth. Authority works when believers know who they are, where they are seated, and whose name they bear.

When the Church remembers this, darkness does not need to be chased—it collapses at the sound of aligned authority.

ACTIVATION

Father, in the name of Jesus, I thank You that I have been made alive together with Christ and that I share in His resurrection life. I decree and declare that I am a new creation in Christ, and as He is, so am I in this world. I declare that because I am in Christ, I have dominion in this life under His lordship. I command everything in my life that is out of alignment with heaven to come into order now. I rebuke every demonic power that has been resisting my destiny and inheritance in the name of Jesus. Today, I take authority over every spirit that has fought against my identity, and I break every false identity and orphan spirit that has tried to hinder me from walking in the fullness of my sonship. I declare that I am seated in heavenly places with Christ. I am filled with the Holy Spirit and empowered by the life of God. I decree that every satanic power is under my feet. Every work of the enemy opposing my life, I trample now in the name of Jesus. You are defeated, and I am victorious because I am in Christ. I take my rightful place as a king and priest in the Kingdom of God, walking in authority, intimacy, and obedience to Him.

CHAPTER 2

LIVING IN THE FULLNESS OF THE SPIRIT

The Apostle Paul stands as a compelling pattern for apostles—and indeed all believers—to follow today. His life and ministry were marked by extraordinary works for the Kingdom of God. Through him, the dead were raised, and God performed unusual miracles, even using handkerchiefs that had touched Paul's body as instruments of healing. Beyond signs and wonders, Paul was entrusted with profound spiritual insight; he authored a significant portion of the New Testament and walked in a level of revelation few have ever known.

So great were the revelations given to him that God permitted a thorn in his flesh—a messenger of satan—to remain, lest Paul be exalted above measure. By his own testimony, he was caught up into realms where he saw and heard things that were "unlawful" or impossible for a human being to fully articulate on earth—realities that transcended the laws of the natural world. Simply put, Paul lived and ministered in the fullness of the Spirit.

What makes Paul's life even more remarkable is that he was never discipled by Jesus in the flesh, as the original apostles were. Yet, in the eyes of many, he stands among—if not above—the greatest of them. His formation did not come through walking beside Christ during His earthly ministry, but through a supernatural discipleship by the Holy Spirit. In this, Paul becomes profoundly relevant to believers today. Like him, we are taught, shaped, and empowered not by physical proximity to Jesus, but by the living work of the Spirit. Paul's life testifies that intimacy with God, depth of revelation, and apostolic impact are not limited by circumstance but are made available through wholehearted surrender to the Spirit's teaching and power.

In order to come into fullness, we must understand several key dynamics of our relationship with the Holy Spirit. This journey unfolds in distinct stages, each building upon the last. These stages are not separate spirits, nor are they optional experiences; they are progressive realities of one Spirit working within the believer. First, we are sealed by the Spirit. Second, we are filled with—or baptized in—the Spirit. Third, we are enlightened by the Spirit. Finally, we learn to walk in the Spirit, fully aware of our inheritance as mature sons. Before breaking each of these down, an important distinction must be made—one that will correct a widespread misunderstanding in the body of Christ.

Once a believer has received the indwelling of the Holy Spirit, the goal is not to get more of the Holy Spirit. Rather, the true focus of the believer is to grow in relationship with the Holy Spirit and to develop and mature the inner man. The Holy Spirit does not arrive in portions, stages, or fragments. He comes in fullness from the very beginning. He does not grow, increase, or evolve. We do.

This shift in understanding is foundational. Many believers unconsciously operate with the assumption that power comes from accumulating more spiritual experiences, more anointing, or more impartations. In reality, power is released through maturity, not accumulation. When this perspective changes, it unlocks a deeper flow of heaven's power through the believer. Many look at others accomplishing great exploits for the Kingdom and assume they possess something different or superior. Yet the same Spirit empowering the ones they admire is the very Spirit dwelling within them. The difference is not the Spirit—it is development. It is the transition from spiritual adolescence to sonship maturity.

SEALED BY THE SPIRIT

To be sealed by the Holy Spirit is to be marked as belonging to God. This sealing takes place at salvation and speaks of identity, ownership, and security. The Spirit becomes the divine seal that confirms we are in Christ and that we have been set apart for God's purposes.

This seal is not merely a future guarantee of heaven; it is a present reality of sonship. The Spirit bears witness with our spirit that we are children of God. At this stage, the believer is made alive spiritually, but much of their thinking, desires, and reactions are still shaped by the soul and the flesh. The seal establishes who we are, even before we fully understand what we carry.

FILLED OR BAPTIZED IN THE SPIRIT

The filling—or baptism—of the Holy Spirit speaks to empowerment. While the Spirit dwells within the believer at salvation, the baptism of the Spirit immerses the believer into divine power for witness, ministry, and supernatural operation. This experience awakens the believer to the realm of the Spirit. Gifts are activated, boldness increases, and spiritual sensitivity begins to grow. However, being filled with the Spirit does not automatically produce maturity. Power without formation can lead to instability. This is why many operate in genuine gifts yet struggle with consistency, character, or discernment.

The baptism of the Spirit is not the destination—it is the doorway. In the next chapter, I will also cover the subject of speaking in tongues to explain how and why every believer should pray in other tongues. This prayer language is imparted onto your spirit at your baptism in the Spirit. Satan does not want believers to speak in tongues—because it is far too powerful for him to tolerate. It is one of the great realities of the New Covenant, something the prophets and people of the Old Covenant never possessed. Even when Isaiah prophesied it, he never experienced it himself. Tongues flow from the inner man, reborn and alive in Christ, and operate from a realm the enemy cannot access.

ENLIGHTENED BY THE SPIRIT

To be enlightened by the Spirit is to have the eyes of the heart opened by wisdom and revelation in the knowledge of God. Scripture says, "*That the God of our Lord Jesus Christ, the Father of glory, may give to you the spirit of wisdom and revelation in the knowledge of Him, the eyes of your understanding being enlightened*" (Ephesians 1:17–18 NKJV). A person who has been enlightened is a person who has been flooded with light. In the realm of the Spirit, light is not merely illumination—it is spirit-knowledge, understanding that comes from God Himself. This is one of the reasons God does not desire that we be filled with the Spirit yet remain ignorant. Spiritual fullness without revelation produces limitation. When we have light in an area of God's Kingdom, we gain the ability to walk in that realm. This is why the psalmist says, "*Your word is a lamp to my feet and a light to my path*" (Psalm 119:105 NKJV). The Word of God makes the ways of God visible, and that visibility gives us the capacity to move, function, and advance in what God has made available. You cannot walk accurately in what you cannot see.

Whenever you observe someone consistently walking in demonstrations of the Spirit's power—whether in faith, authority, healing, discernment, or dominion—it is not accidental. It is the result of the revelation and wisdom that the person possesses. They have light. Jesus taught this principle in Matthew 6 when He said, "*The lamp of the body is the eye. If therefore your eye is good, your whole body will be full of light. But if your eye is bad, your whole body will be full of darkness...*" (Matthew 6:22–23 NKJV). What enters through perception determines what fills the entire life. When we look at the wrong things or carry the wrong perception, we end up filling ourselves with the darkness we see and meditate on. This reveals that sight was designed by God not only as a means to see but also to receive.

Whenever God desires to give something to a person, that person must first be able to see it. This is why God reveals things through His Word, through visions, and through dreams. He is not merely informing us—He is imparting light. Scripture says, "*Where there is no vision, the people perish...*" (Proverbs 29:18 KJV). Vision is not optional; it is the gateway of inheritance. Everything that comes from the Spirit begins as light, and through faith, that light becomes material in the physical world. "*By faith we understand that the worlds were framed by the word of God, so that the things which are seen were not made of things which are visible*" (Hebrews 11:3 NKJV). This is why in Genesis God began creation with light, declaring, "...*Let there be light*" (Genesis 1:3 NKJV) before anything else took form. Revelation always precedes manifestation.

God desires to make you the light of the world—a person filled with divine knowledge that can be manifested as proof of His Kingdom. Jesus said, "*You are the light of the world... Let your light so shine before men, that they may see your good works and glorify your Father in heaven*" (Matthew 5:14, 16 NKJV). In Hebrews, the writer outlines the elementary principles of Christ and then urges believers to move beyond foundational truths into maturity. As the passage continues, maturity is described as being enlightened, and the result of that enlightenment is *tasting "the powers of the age to come"* (Hebrews 6:4-5 NKJV). The age to come refers to the future Kingdom reality—when satan is bound, when heaven and earth are fully joined in Christ, and when the body of Christ walks in immortality. Yet Scripture reveals that the powers of that age can be tasted now, in this present life. However, this realm is not accessed by believers who remain unenlightened.

Revelation is the bridge between the present age and the age to come. Without light, believers remain confined to survival Christianity. With light, they begin to access Kingdom realities ahead of time. God is not withholding power; He is calling His people into enlightenment. Where light comes, dominion follows.

WALKING IN THE SPIRIT AS MATURE SONS

Walking in the Spirit is the fruit of maturity. It is the state in which the believer no longer lives driven by impulses, emotions, or external pressures, but by inward union with the

Spirit of God. Scripture declares, *"If we live in the Spirit, let us also walk in the Spirit"* (Galatians 5:25 NKJV). This walk is not merely a spiritual activity; it is spiritual governance. It is marked by discernment, self-rule, obedience, and authority because the believer has learned how to yield their inner life to the Spirit rather than being mastered by the flesh. *"For as many as are led by the Spirit of God, these are sons of God"* (Romans 8:14 NKJV). Being led is evidence of sonship, not gifting.

An immature believer may often feel as though the things promised in the Word are distant, unattainable, or reserved for others. They read about authority, peace, power, inheritance, and victory, yet experience life as though these realities are not in their possession. This is not because the Word is untrue, but because immaturity limits access. Scripture is clear: *"...His divine power has given to us all things that pertain to life and godliness, through the knowledge of Him..."* (2 Peter 1:3 NKJV). The problem is never supply—it is development. Everything has already been granted in Christ, but only maturity allows a believer to walk in what has already been given.

This is why Paul says, *"...The heir, as long as he is a child, does not differ at all from a slave, though he is master of all"* (Galatians 4:1 NKJV). The child owns everything by right yet enjoys nothing by experience. Immaturity creates the illusion of lack in the middle of abundance. Mature sons, however, are aware of their inheritance. They do not strive for identity; they minister from it. They do not chase power; they steward what has already been entrusted to them. They are not impressed by the flesh, not governed by fear, and not manipulated by circumstances because they have learned to discern spiritual realities over natural appearances. *"...He who is spiritual judges all things..."* (1 Corinthians 2:15 NKJV).

This is the realm where exploits flow naturally—not because the believer is seeking greatness, but because heaven trusts them with influence. Daniel 11:32 (NKJV) declares, "*...The people who know their God shall be strong and carry out great exploits.*" Exploits are not the pursuit of ambition; they are the byproduct of intimacy and obedience. Authority is released where alignment exists, and power is entrusted—where character can contain it.

Scripture explains this developmental process through the doctrine of adoption. One of the primary titles given to the Holy Spirit is "*...the Spirit of adoption*" (Romans 8:15 NKJV). Adoption in the biblical sense is not about God deciding to love us later; it is about God placing trained sons into authority. In the Roman world, adoption referred to the public installation of a mature son into office. A son could be born into a household but remain under tutors and governors until the appointed time of maturity. "*Even so we, when we were children, were in bondage under the elements of the world. But when the fullness of the time had come, God sent forth His Son...to redeem those under the law, that we might receive the adoption as sons*" (Galatians 4:3-5 NKJV). Adoption was the moment when limitation was removed, and authority was conferred.

This means a believer can be born again, Spirit-filled, and yet not walking in fullness—not because God is withholding, but because maturity has not yet produced placement. The Spirit of adoption does not merely assure us that we belong. He trains us until heaven can entrust us. Placement follows formation. Authority follows self-governance. Inheritance follows sonship. "*If children, then heirs—heirs of God and joint heirs with Christ*" (Romans 8:17 NKJV), but heirs only function in what they are mature enough to steward.

This is where the Word of God plays its critical role. Scripture is not only informative; it is formative. The Word does not simply reveal inheritance—it builds the believer into the capacity to walk in it. Paul declares, "*And now, brethren, I commend you to God and to the word of His grace, which is able to build you up and give you an inheritance among all those who are sanctified*" (Acts 20:32 NKJV). The Word builds us up into maturity, and maturity unlocks inheritance. You do not grow into inheritance by time; you grow into it by truth.

Walking in the Spirit, then, is not mystical; it's governmental. It is the life of a son who has been trained, disciplined, and aligned with the Father's will, just as Jesus Himself was. "*Though He was a Son, yet He learned obedience by the things which He suffered*" (Hebrews 5:8 NKJV). Adoption is not sentimental; it's positional. And when sons are placed, heaven entrusts them with the powers of the age to come, not because they demanded them, but because they are ready to carry them. That is the walk of the Spirit. That is the journey from inheritance promised to inheritance possessed. And that is how the Kingdom advances—not through striving, but through sons who have been built up by the Word and placed by the Spirit into office.

The Holy Spirit living within us is the divine reality that brings about our union with Jesus Christ and with the Father. This union is not partial, progressive, or distant—it is complete. Once you receive the Holy Spirit, you cannot become any closer to God than you already are in your spirit. Scripture tells us that when we are joined to the Lord, we become one spirit with Him. There is no intimacy beyond oneness.

Many believers assume that death will somehow bring them into a deeper relationship with God. Yet eternal life does not begin when we leave this world; it begins the moment

God regenerates our spirit. Eternal life is not merely a future destination; it is a present reality. What we experience now through the indwelling Holy Spirit is the beginning of that life which continues unbroken into eternity.

When we eventually graduate from this life and enter heaven, we are not starting something new; we are continuing what has already begun. And when Jesus returns, and the new earth is established, we will live once again on earth—this time in fullness and glory. The relationship we cultivate now with the Holy Spirit is therefore profoundly significant because it reflects how we will walk with Him in the age to come.

The Holy Spirit is Lord, and His primary assignment is on the earth. He is not distant or passive but actively involved in our lives. He speaks—not on His own authority, but what He hears. He searches the deep things of God and makes them known to us. He teaches us, leads us, and guides us into all truth. He reveals what is to come and continually points our hearts and understanding back to Jesus.

Life in the Spirit, then, is not about striving to get closer to God, but about learning to live from the closeness we already possess. As we grow in awareness and cooperation with the Holy Spirit, what is already true in our spirit increasingly becomes evident in our daily walk. To understand more fully the Holy Spirit's function within us, we must understand the many ways He manifests His presence and how He works in our lives. Scripture refers to these manifestations as the seven Spirits of God. This does not describe seven different spirits, nor stages of spiritual access, but the sevenfold fullness of the one Holy Spirit operating in completeness.

Some have taught that after a believer receives the baptism of the Holy Spirit, the seven Spirits become available only if one later "presses in" for more. This is inaccurate. When you received the baptism of the Holy Spirit, you were immersed—submerged—into the fullness of God. You did not receive a partial measure. You received all of Him. The seven Spirits are not something added later; they describe the supernatural ways the Holy Spirit already works within you.

Scripture reveals this sevenfold expression as the Spirit of the LORD, wisdom, understanding, counsel, might, knowledge, and the fear of the LORD. Because we are joined to Christ, the same Spirit that rested upon Him now dwells within us (see Isaiah 11:2). These manifestations unfold in daily life as the Spirit leads us—establishing identity through the Spirit of the LORD, shaping perception through wisdom and understanding, directing paths through counsel, strengthening endurance through might, revealing truth through knowledge, and anchoring our hearts in reverence through the fear of the LORD. These are not separate experiences to chase, but dimensions of the Spirit already present, made visible through obedience and relationship.

Scripture also reveals the Holy Spirit as the seven Spirits before the throne of God (see Revelation 1:4). This imagery shows the Spirit in His governmental fullness—ready to carry out the will of God throughout the earth. The significance for the believer is profound: the Spirit who stands before the throne is the same Spirit who lives within us. Heaven's authority is not distant; it is meant to be expressed through yielded lives on earth.

These seven Spirits are further described as the seven eyes of the Lord. Zechariah 4:10 (NIV) says that the seven eyes of the Lord *"range throughout the earth,"* and Revelation 5:6 (NKJV) identifies these eyes as *"...the seven Spirits of God sent out into all the earth."* This speaks of perfect sight, discernment, and awareness. The Holy Spirit searches all things—even the deep things of God—and makes them known to us. In the believer, this manifests as spiritual perception: discernment of truth and error, sensitivity to God's movement, and insight beyond natural understanding.

Believers themselves are described as living stones, which explains how this heavenly reality becomes personal and tangible. First Peter 2:5 (NIV) declares that we are "... *living stones...being built into a spiritual house....*" We are living because the Spirit lives within us. Each stone carries life, not from itself, but from the indwelling Holy Spirit. The sevenfold Spirit does not divide Himself among believers; He fully indwells each one, while expressing Himself uniquely through each life.

Jesus Himself is the cornerstone of this house. Ephesians explains that we are being fit together upon Christ to become a dwelling place of God in the Spirit (see Ephesians 2:19–22 (NKJV). Because the sevenfold Spirit rested upon Christ, and because we are joined to Him, that same Spirit now rests upon us. As living stones, we are intentionally placed, aligned, and joined together so that God may dwell among His people.

This means that what exists before the throne is now present in the temple—and the temple is no longer a building, but a people. Each believer becomes a mobile dwelling place of God, carrying heaven's wisdom, authority, discernment, and power into everyday life. Individually, we are filled with His fullness; corporately, we reveal His habitation.

The seven Spirits of God, then, are not about striving for more of God, but about yielding to the fullness already within us. What governs heaven now empowers life on earth. As we learn to live from this reality, the house of God becomes visible in the world—alive, discerning, ordered, and filled with glory—now, and in the age to come.

ACTIVATION

Father, in Jesus' name, I thank You for the Holy Spirit. I thank You that He lives in me, that He comforts me, that He helps me, and that He is my friend. Right now, I come against any religious spirit that would try to keep me from partnering with the work and moving of the Holy Spirit inside me. I thank You that I am filled with all the fullness of God and that the seven Spirits of God are manifesting in my life right now.

Lord, I repent for any way I may have grieved You or extinguished Your fire in my life, Holy Spirit. I ask You right now, in the same way that You empowered Christ, I thank You that You have empowered me. I thank You that I am close with You, that You are in me, and that You are flowing through my life. I decree and declare right now that I am not an ordinary man, because I am filled with the same Spirit that raised Christ from the dead.

CHAPTER 3

ALIGNING WITH HEAVEN THROUGH PRAYING IN THE SPIRIT

Rivers are flowing! A pastor shouted these words into a microphone as I received the baptism of the Spirit. An unknown language was flowing from my mouth, and even though I didn't understand it, I could feel so much life, peace, and God's presence. That moment meant so much to me because I had been seeking God for months about the baptism of the Spirit, and I had become discouraged. I searched everywhere for the baptism. I traveled all around the city looking for someone who could help me receive this baptism, and I kept returning to the water for baptism again and again. I even went to an old-school church and had someone lead me in tarrying for the Holy Spirit. I said "Hallelujah," over and over. I said "Jesus" repeatedly, but I did not receive the baptism of the Spirit. I was told that I must have sin in my life, which was why I hadn't received the baptism of the Spirit. Being young in the faith, hearing this truly affected me, but now I know that it was a complete lie. We do not receive the Holy Spirit as a reward, but as a gift that empowers us to live spiritually.

The Sunday I was filled with the Spirit, I went up to the altar during an altar call. They weren't even praying for that, but I was so hungry for God that when I reached the front, one of the church elders prayed for me. As he prayed, the power of God hit me, and I was filled with the Spirit almost instantly. I never realized that, according to Acts chapter 19, the easiest and fastest way for someone to be filled with the Spirit is for hands to be laid on them specifically for that. After that day, everything about my life changed completely. I was filled with power, and I saw an immediate transformation in my prayer life. My ability to seek God in prayer improved dramatically—I became much more sensitive to Him. I was more aware of His presence even when I read the Bible. I understood the Word of God differently, and I began to experience God using me through the gifts of the Spirit to truly be a witness of Jesus Christ.

It requires us to move in the power of God. There's nothing wrong with character, and we absolutely need character, but the two were never meant to oppose each other. There was never supposed to be a group in the church that said I am part of the character tribe and another group that says I'm part of the power tribe. In the book of Acts, every believer walked in the power of God. There is no biblical pattern of a New Testament believer who does not have the power of God flowing in their life. When it comes to cancer, disease, the dead being raised, or blind eyes, character alone will not cause these things to change. Character alone does not release miracles. You can go to a church where the pastor is a kind person but doesn't believe in the power of God, and if sickness gets into your body, you could die prematurely, even though the pastor is very welcoming and kind. Jesus went about doing good by the power of the Holy Spirit that was in His life, and this is the primary thing we receive when we are baptized in the Spirit: we receive power.

In the Word of God, we see two primary baptisms that shape the life of the believer: the baptism in water and the baptism in the Holy Spirit. Both are essential, both are powerful, and both reveal different dimensions of our union with Christ.

Water baptism is the baptism of identification. It is the outward expression of an inward faith that says, "I am united with Jesus Christ." When we go down into the water, we are declaring by faith that we have died with Him. Just as Christ bore our sin and the weight of fallen humanity on the cross, our old man—the person we were in Adam—is counted as crucified with Him. This is not symbolic only in an emotional sense; it is a spiritual reality. Scripture teaches that our old self was crucified with Christ so that the body ruled by sin would lose its power. When we are raised up out of the water, we are declaring that we have been raised with Christ into newness of life. From God's point of view, we are no longer defined by who we were in the fall, but by who Jesus is in His resurrection.

This is the miracle of union. When Jesus died, we died in Him. When He was buried, our old life was buried with Him. When He rose from the dead, He did not rise only as an individual, but as the head of a new creation. We rose with Him into that new creation reality. Now we are patterned after the resurrected Christ. We share in His victory, His righteousness, and His standing before the Father. Scripture even says we are seated with Him in heavenly places. That means our spiritual position has changed completely. We are no longer trying to reach God from a place of distance; we live from a place of union, authority, and acceptance. Water baptism proclaims this finished work. It announces that we have crossed from death into life and that our identity is now rooted in the resurrected Christ.

But the baptism in the Holy Spirit differs in purpose and experience. Water baptism symbolizes identification with Christ's death and resurrection. The baptism in the Holy Spirit, however, is about empowerment for Christ's mission. In water baptism, we are united with Christ. In Spirit baptism, the Spirit is poured out upon and within us in a way that fills, overflows, and empowers us.

This is when the Holy Spirit comes to dwell within us and clothes us with power from on high. Jesus told His disciples, who already believed in Him and had received His breath of life, to wait until they were endued with power from heaven. The baptism in the Holy Spirit is not about becoming saved; it is about becoming empowered. It is the difference between having life and having power flowing through that life. When the Holy Spirit fills a believer, He brings boldness, spiritual language, heightened sensitivity to God, and the activation of spiritual gifts. The same Spirit who raised Jesus from the dead begins to operate through us, not just to transform our character but to release the works of God through our lives.

Through this baptism, prayer becomes deeper, worship becomes more alive, and the Scriptures open with greater clarity. We become witnesses in demonstration, not just in words. The power of the Spirit enables us to heal the sick, cast out demons, prophesy, and reveal Jesus to the world in a tangible way. It is heaven's empowerment for earthly assignment.

Water baptism establishes our identity in the death and resurrection of Christ, marking the end of the old life and the beginning of the new. Paul went on to say, *"I thank my God, I speak with tongues more than you all"* (1 Corinthians 14:18 NKJV), speaking to the church in Corinth. He also said, *"I will pray with the spirit, and I will also pray with the understanding"* (1 Corinthians 14:15 NKJV). This shows that when Paul prayed, one of his primary means of communion with God was in an unknown tongue. Praying in an unknown tongue brings us into a place where we speak to God, spirit to Spirit.

I remember a time when I was ministering in Puerto Rico during very powerful meetings. They assigned someone to me as an interpreter. This person would speak in my ear while others were ministering who spoke only Spanish. At one point, my interpreter had to step away briefly to take care of something. The moment the interpreter left, I was completely disconnected from what was happening around me. Even though I was physically present, I could not understand anything. In that moment, the importance of communication in the same language became very clear.

This is what speaking in tongues does. It allows you to fully express yourself to God and breaks the limitations of natural language. When we pray in the Spirit, we pray above our understanding. There are times when our understanding can hinder our ability to pray in faith or even to pray the right prayer. But God has given us this supernatural language so we can pray according to what is on His heart and in His mind.

As you begin to speak in other tongues, a direct line of communication and fellowship between your spirit, the Holy Spirit, and the mind of God begins to flow. Everything you pray out of your spirit comes from divine inspiration—an impartation from God Himself. This practice does not originate in the mind, and this is what the Bible means when it says, *"For if I pray in a tongue, my spirit prays, but my understanding is unfruitful*" (1 Corinthians 14:14 NKJV). When Paul says the mind is unfruitful, he is not saying this kind of prayer is unhelpful. He is explaining that it bypasses the limitations of the mind and allows you to pray with the faith of God—the same faith that brought the world into existence, the same faith that spoke to deaf ears and caused them to hear.

By bypassing the mind and flowing directly out of your spirit, doubt and unbelief are removed from what comes out of your mouth. The benefits of this gift cannot truly be measured. Paul also mentioned singing in the Spirit (1 Corinthians 14:15 NKJV). We can sing in the Spirit just as we pray in the Spirit. As we lift our voices and sing in other tongues, we begin to worship from that same place within, offering praise that flows directly out of our inner man. We speak the wonderful works of God in a language given by the Spirit.

There are times when I sing in the Spirit, and I have found that it becomes a shortcut into the glory realm. When I remain there, resting in that flow, the sense of God's presence continues to increase as I sing in tongues. Scripture supports this reality. Isaiah prophesied about this experience long before the New Covenant, saying, *"For with stammering lips and another tongue will He speak to this people. To whom He said, 'This is the rest with which you may cause the weary to rest,' and 'This is the refreshing'..."* (Isaiah 28:11–12 NKJV). What Isaiah saw prophetically, we now experience personally. Praying and singing in tongues brings spiritual rest and refreshing to the inner man.

Recently, phone companies introduced what they call a "fast charger." It can charge a device's battery to a high percentage in a short amount of time. I still have an older charger, and when I use it, it takes much longer for my phone's battery to gain any real charge. That contrast helps me understand what praying in the Spirit does. It is like a spiritual fast charger for the inner man. Jude writes, *"But you, beloved, building up yourselves on your most holy faith, praying in the Holy Spirit"* (Jude 1:20 NKJV). When we pray in tongues, we are spiritually building ourselves up—charging our spirit like a battery being filled with power.

As we pray in the Spirit, we are filled with God's strength. We are refreshed and renewed. We receive fresh impartation from the Holy Spirit. New fire begins to stir within our inner man, and at times, that overflow can even affect our physical body with renewed strength and endurance. Just as a fast charger quickly restores power to a drained device, praying in tongues restores spiritual vitality to a weary believer.

If you spend consistent time praying in other tongues, burnout begins to lose its grip. Weakness is replaced with spiritual strength. Weariness gives way to divine refreshment. This is exactly what Isaiah was pointing to when he connected "another tongue" with rest and refreshing. Praying in the Spirit is not empty repetition—it is supernatural renewal flowing from direct communion with God. Praying in tongues does more than edify the individual believer—it stirs the entire spirit life and helps activate sensitivity to the gifts of the Spirit. When you consistently pray in the Spirit, your inner man becomes more responsive to the Holy Spirit's movements. It is like clearing spiritual static so you can more clearly perceive His promptings, impressions, and leadings. The gifts of the Spirit are not mechanical abilities we switch on at will; they flow through yielded, spiritually aware vessels. Praying in tongues strengthens that awareness and keeps the spirit man active, alert, and receptive.

Scripture says, *"But you, beloved, building up yourselves on your most holy faith, praying in the Holy Spirit"* (Jude 1:20

NKJV). This "most holy faith" is not just personal belief—it is the same faith demonstrated by the saints who walked with God before us, the faith we see expressed throughout the New Testament, and the faith rooted in the promises of the Old. It is the living, supernatural faith that trusts God, acts on His Word, and expects Him to move. When Jude speaks of building ourselves up in this faith, he is pointing to strengthening our capacity to live in the same spiritual reality they walked in.

Elsewhere, Scripture talks about "*...the faith which was once for all delivered to the saints*" (Jude 1:3). This means the faith is to be passed on unchanged—not reduced, not explained away, and not stripped of its supernatural dimension. A lifestyle of praying in tongues helps preserve that original faith in experience, not just in doctrine. It keeps the believer connected to the same power, dependence, and expectancy that marked the early Church.

A commitment to praying in the Spirit will gradually draw you into a life where biblical realities become normal. The more you pray in tongues, the more your spirit becomes aligned with heaven's perspective, and the more natural it becomes to step out in obedience when the Spirit prompts you. Faith grows stronger, boldness increases, and spiritual gifts have room to operate. What once felt intimidating begins to feel like a natural outflow of your relationship with God.

Over time, people begin to see the fruit of that life. They see prayers answered, wisdom beyond natural ability, peace in pressure, love in difficult situations, and sometimes even supernatural intervention. Your life becomes a testimony that the Word of God is not just history—it is present reality. People begin to recognize that Jesus is alive, not merely because of what you say, but because of what flows through your life. The goal is never to impress people, but to reveal Christ. And praying in the Spirit is one of the ways the Holy Spirit prepares and strengthens a believer to live as a visible expression of an invisible Kingdom.

ACTIVATION

Father, I thank You for giving me divine tongues. I thank You that, as I pray in tongues, things are being settled in the spirit in my favor—chaos and demonic activity are being rebuked and arrested as I pray in my heavenly languages. I believe that I have the top angels, as angels are moving into action to minister to me. I believe that all the mysteries that are being spoken about as I pray right now, Lord, are for the manifestation of my prayers. As I pray in tongues right now, Lord, I ask You to give me the ability to interpret because, Lord, in interpretation there will be answers to what I have been asking You. You are giving me ideas, You're opening doors to businesses, You're manifesting divine power, and You are exposing the words of darkness as I pray in another tongue. Amen.

Now I encourage praying in tongues for at least one hour a day.

CHAPTER 4

LIVING IN RESURRECTION POWER

Scripture tells us that the same power that raised Jesus from the dead now dwells in us, and that power gives life even to our mortal bodies. This truth is far bigger than just miracles, signs, and wonders—though it certainly includes them. It reaches into the reality of divine life flowing through the believer here and now. Yes, the outward man is aging and fading, but there is a realm of resurrection life on the inside of you that does not decay. That life can strengthen your body, renew your inner being, and cause the life of the Spirit to flow into your physical frame.

This resurrection life is not only about physical vitality; it speaks of the entirely new life we have entered because Christ has risen from the dead. When Jesus came out of the grave, He stepped into a new order of life, and as those who are born again, we share in that same life. From God's perspective, you are no longer just a natural person trying to survive in a broken world. You are a new creation, joined to the risen Christ, carrying resurrection reality on the inside of you. There is nothing ordinary about a born-again believer. Heaven's life has taken up residence in an earthly vessel.

The foundation of living in resurrection power is understanding what it truly means to be born again. Being born again is not merely adopting new beliefs or turning over a new leaf; it is receiving a new nature and a new source of life. The Spirit of God unites you with the risen Christ, and His victory becomes your starting point. This is why resurrection is not just a future event we are waiting for—it is the definition of the life we now live. Eternal life is not only about living forever; it is about sharing in the quality of life that belongs to the risen Son of God.

When you begin to see yourself this way, your expectations change. You stop seeing yourself as weak, limited, and merely human, and you begin to recognize that the Spirit who conquered death lives in you. That resurrection life works in your spirit, transforms your mind, and can even affect your body. You are not trying to reach resurrection one day; you are learning to live from resurrection today.

> Therefore, we were buried with Him through baptism into death, that just as Christ was raised from the dead by the glory of the Father, even so we also should walk in newness of life (Romans 6:4 NKJV).

This is the clearest statement that we were raised with Christ to live a new life. Though the verse we referenced is about baptism—which we covered in the previous chapter—I want to draw your attention to the emphasis that the glory of the Father raised Christ, and that "*...even so we also should walk in newness of life*" (Romans 6:4 NKJV). That word is also important. It tells us that just as Christ entered a new kind of life through resurrection, we are now called to live in that same quality of life. If we are going to understand the life we now have, we must understand the life of the resurrected Christ. When Christ rose from the dead, He rose with all power and authority, as we discussed in chapter two. But Scripture makes it clear that something about Him was different. In Luke 24, two disciples who had known Him before walked with Him on the road to Emmaus and did not recognize Him. This detail is not random. It reveals that while Jesus was still truly Himself, He had entered a glorified, resurrected state of life. His humanity was now clothed with resurrection glory.

Another powerful moment happened when Mary Magdalene encountered the risen Jesus near the tomb. At first, she thought He was the gardener. It was only when He spoke her name that her eyes were opened and she recognized Him. Again, this shows us that there was both continuity and transformation. He was the same Jesus, yet now living in a new, glorified order of life.

Jesus rose during the Feast of Firstfruits, and this timing was deeply significant. Firstfruits was an offering that represented the beginning of a harvest still to come. Christ rose as the firstfruits because He is the head of a new creation—the first of an entirely new kind of humanity. His resurrection was not just a miracle; it marked the start of a new creation reality.

Before Jesus, there were resurrections recorded in Scripture, but each one was temporary. Lazarus was raised from the dead, yet he eventually died again. The little girl Jesus raised also returned to mortal life and later faced death. These resurrections were powerful signs, but they were restorations to natural life, still under the shadow of death, because the reign of sin and death had not yet been fully broken.

When Jesus came out of the grave, everything changed. He did not rise mortal—He rose immortal. Death no longer had authority over Him. Sin, the grave, and the curse had no hold. Scripture says that death no longer has dominion over Him. In His new life, He cannot die again. He lives in resurrection glory, and that life is now the pattern for the new life we are called to walk in. So what is available in our new life breaks the dominion of death. When people think about death, they think only of physically dying. Death is a spirit, and its fruit can manifest in any area that God created. Death can work in your body, your marriage, your finances and business, your relationships, your dreams, and your destiny. Our new life causes us to come out of the dominion of death and live in the realm of life. Death comes to anything under the dominion of satan. So think of death as a realm. Our salvation gives us the ability to live above that realm of death.

In our next chapter, I will be breaking down in detail how to stay in the realm of life. For now, I will explain what it means in scripture for us when it says that to be carnally minded is death, but to be spiritually minded is life and peace. So this means our meditation on the things of God and His Kingdom determines which realm we experience the most of. To think carnally will give authority to death in whatever area our thinking is not in agreement with God. To unlock the resurrection power in you, there must be agreement with God. This is why in Ezekiel 37 (NKJV), when God took the prophet Ezekiel into the valley of dry bones, the Lord asked Ezekiel if the very bones could live. Though this is easy to gloss over, God asking a mere man a question must be considered deeply.

Why would an all-knowing God need to ask Ezekiel if the bones could live? It's because God never did anything in this text. Ezekiel spoke to the winds. Ezekiel spoke to the bones. The four winds heard the voice of Ezekiel and began to blow. These winds brought resurrection life to the dry bones. Though resurrection is in you already, it can be dormant due to a lack of agreement with God. If Ezekiel had not believed that the bones could live again, God would have had to find another voice to speak to the winds. In this resurrection life, we must understand that we are like Him in the resurrection.

This means that everything Christ inherited from the Father, He now shares with us as our inheritance. Scripture says we are "*...heirs of God and joint heirs with Christ*" (Romans 8:17 NKJV). What belongs to the Son by right now belongs to us by grace because we are in Him. On earth, we are called to reflect who He is in heaven, for "*...as He is, so are we in this world*" (1 John 4:17 NKJV). This is not arrogance—it is covenant reality.

We see a shadow of this mystery in the story of Esau and Jacob. When Isaac was old and near death, it was time to pass on the inheritance. In Jewish culture, the firstborn son received the double portion, meaning a greater share of the inheritance and blessing (see Deuteronomy 21:17). If a father had three portions, the older son would receive two and the younger one would receive one. By birth, Esau was the rightful heir to the double portion.

Yet when the time came to release the blessing, Rebekah instructed Jacob to clothe himself in Esau's garments and cover his smooth skin so that he would feel like his hairy brother. Because Isaac's eyesight was weak, he blessed Jacob, believing he was Esau (see Genesis 27). While this story includes human weakness and deception, it also prophetically illustrates a spiritual truth: Jacob received the blessing because he came in the likeness of the firstborn.

In the New Covenant, there is no lesser and greater inheritance among sons. There is only the fullness of the inheritance in Christ. Jesus is called "*...the firstborn among many brethren*" (Romans 8:29 NKJV), and He has received the full inheritance from the Father. But we are in Him. We have been clothed in Christ (see Galatians 3:27), and we now stand before the Father in His likeness. Because of this, the glory, the spiritual blessings, and the authority that belong to Christ now belong to us in Him. Scripture says God "*...has blessed us with every spiritual blessing in the heavenly places in Christ*" (Ephesians 1:3 NKJV).

With this foundation, we must also understand that your life is now the continuation of Christ's life on the earth. This is what Paul meant when he said, "*It is no longer I who live, but Christ lives in me*" (Galatians 2:20 NKJV). You are a new creation (see 2 Corinthians 5:17), made a partaker of the divine nature (see 2 Peter 1:4), carrying the very life of God within you.

Jesus described this union by saying, "*I am the vine, you are the branches. He who abides in Me, and I in him, bears much fruit...*" (John 15:5 NKJV). The life that flows through the vine is the same life that flows into the branches. It is not a different life or a lesser life—it is the same life. That divine life produces in us the same kind of fruit that was seen in Christ, because it is His life continuing to express itself through us.

I was ministering in Atlanta, Georgia, at a Spiritual Sons and Daughters church. As I was teaching, I could feel the power of Christ's resurrection flowing through me. When I began to minister to the sick, creative miracles and deliverance started happening. One person was healed of scoliosis, and then another. A cancerous tumor vanished from a woman's breast. God's power was evident. Short limbs were growing, bones were being realigned, and suddenly, we began to hear a woman screaming.

At first, I assumed she was going through deliverance. But then someone ran to tell my assistant that a five-year-old girl who had been nonverbal had just spoken her first words in the glory. Those words were "Hallelujah!" The little girl was shouting praise to God. His glory completely overcame us.

These kinds of things become normal when we understand that the resurrection life of Jesus lives in us. You do not have to be an apostle, a prophet, or have a global ministry to be used in resurrection power. You need to have Jesus living inside you and the Holy Spirit upon you. These miracles can happen through your hands.

I believe God is raising up a generation that will move in the power of God and bring revival to the earth and into their own spheres of influence. We will see entire families saved. We will see glory break out in unusual places, and many people will come to the Lord and be born again because they have witnessed the power of God flowing through ordinary believers—not just through those seen as "special." Resurrection life lives inside every one of us.

It's like in the days of Moses with Eldad and Medad. The Spirit of God came upon them, and they prophesied even though they were not among the recognized elders and were outside the main gathering. Joshua asked Moses if he should stop them, but Moses wisely told him not to. God desired that all His people would carry His Spirit.

Somewhere along the way, it has become embedded in people's hearts that you must have a title, position, or public recognition to be used by God. But the resurrection life of Jesus inside you is the only qualification you need to flow in the power of God and be used to change the world.

ACTIVATION

Father, I thank You that I have been raised into new life right now. In the name of Jesus, the resurrection life of God flows through me and flows into all the dead things and situations in my life. I thank You that nothing can remain dead in me or around me right now, in the name of Jesus. The same Spirit who raised Jesus from the dead quickens my mortal body, and I thank You that my whole body is being touched and quickened by resurrection life right now. I thank You that I have divine health. I thank You that I am an agent of transformation and the miraculous. As a new creation patterned after Jesus Christ, I thank You for His life being lived through me, and that my old life is dead.

CHAPTER 5
THINKING SUPERNATURALLY

One of the primary aspects of living in the Spirit is the renewal of the mind. One of satan's choice weapons against the Church is actually ignorance. On the surface, this may sound harmless, but the Word of God tells us that the just are delivered by knowledge. That means ignorance is not neutral—it keeps people bound.

We have been given all things that pertain to life and godliness. However, we need the intimate knowledge of Jesus to walk as manifested sons. If God places such an emphasis on renewing the mind, it reveals that the mind plays a vital role in unlocking our divine inheritance.

In Ephesians 1, Paul begins to share a prayer he was praying over the church at Ephesus. He prayed that the eyes of their understanding would be flooded with light. First, notice that our eyes and our understanding are connected. But it doesn't stop there. The eyes of our understanding also cause us to access the inheritance that is already inside of us.

Something that's already there becomes touchable when we gain light, which is revelation, knowledge, and insight from the Word of God. This is what Scripture means when it says, "*The entrance of Your words give light*" (Psalm 119:130 NKJV). Light is what makes spiritual realities visible. And once you can truly see, you can walk in what has always been yours.

THE STATE OF THE MIND

There are different conditions the mind can be in. After the fall, all men had a carnal mind. The carnal mind is essentially the mind divorced from the spirit of man. Once Adam ate from the tree, and man's spirit died, his thinking was separated from the mind of God. The way the mind of God is revealed to man is through his spirit.

This is why the Bible says that "*...the spirit of man is the candle of the Lord, searching all the inward parts*" (Proverbs 20:27 KJV). God imparts His Word into our spirit, and from there it is meant to flow into our natural thinking. That process was short-circuited after the fall of man.

The carnal mind is intellectual, reasonable, and humanistic in our time. These things are not evil in themselves, but they are completely opposed to the supernatural realm when they stand alone. In Romans 8 (NKJV), Paul explains that the natural mind cannot understand the things of the Spirit, and thus cannot comprehend God Himself, who is Spirit. The Bible says that the carnal mind is enmity against God. It is not subject to the law of God, nor indeed can it be. So the carnal mind fights and opposes the things of the Spirit when it is disconnected from the spirit of man.

A great example of this is when Paul spoke of being caught up into paradise. He said he saw things that were "unlawful" to utter. He did not mean evil—there is no evil in heaven. He was saying he saw things that go against natural laws. They are unlawful in our world because they contradict the natural order.

The carnal mind can be brilliant in science, in physics, and in things that do not extend beyond the natural realm. But if you have a carnal mind, the extent of your knowledge—no matter how much you gain—cannot tap into the spiritual. When believers have a carnal mind, they cannot unlock the power of heaven because the power of heaven does not follow natural laws. God's power and His glory do not submit to the natural order. In fact, they break it, bend it, and supernaturally override it to bring heaven to earth.

For many years, while being in church, I thought that "carnal" meant people who smoke, drink, and use foul language. But in the Greek, the word *carnal* points to being sensual—sense-ruled. In other words, to be carnal means to live your life based only on what you can see with your natural eyes and hear with your natural ears.

For example, if someone is sick and receives a report from the doctor that they only have a certain amount of time to live, a carnal believer will instantly come into agreement with the doctor's words. In their mind, medical science is the highest form of knowledge, and the natural realm holds the most authority.

Those who are spiritual understand that anything that happens in the natural first begins in the spirit. The spirit realm influences—and in many ways governs—the natural realm. When there is chaos and disunity in the natural, it is often a reflection of spiritual activity. So the way to truly begin changing our lives is to walk in the Spirit. And this requires higher knowledge. This is the knowledge of the glory that the prophet Habakkuk spoke of when he said the whole earth shall be filled with the knowledge of His glory. Another way to describe this is spiritual knowledge.

God is raising up a generation that is not ignorant of spiritual things. As the world shakes around us, we are connected to a Kingdom that cannot be shaken. Having a spiritual mindset is truly building your life on the words of Jesus, so that when the storms come, they cannot shake your house because the foundation is right.

When we do not understand the supernatural, we cannot have a proper foundation. Even Paul said in 1 Corinthians 2 that he did not speak with the wisdom of men, but in demonstration of the Spirit and of power, so that our faith would not stand in the wisdom of men but in the power of God. That means the power of God is meant to be a foundation for faith. Anytime the power of God is not understood or embraced, true faith cannot fully develop, because faith is supernatural. Faith and the power of God go hand in hand.

So there are people not living in sexual immorality and still have a carnal mind because of how they view the supernatural. Any area where we do not agree with the Word of God reveals traces of the carnal mind. Anytime we write off the supernatural that is clearly revealed in Scripture, it is connected to a carnal way of thinking. Our minds are in desperate need of renewal. The next condition of the mind is the renewed mind. When the mind is renewed, all the strongholds are brought down.

What begins to happen in the renewed mind is that truth stops being something we visit occasionally and starts becoming the lens through which we see everything. The renewed mind does not mean we suddenly know everything or never struggle with doubt; it means there is a new default setting forming. Instead of instinctively reacting from fear, pride, or limitation, the heart begins to lean toward trust, humility, and expectation of God's involvement. This is why the transformation Paul speaks of in Romans 12 is tied directly to mind renewal—because without a changed way of thinking, we will keep reproducing the same patterns even while asking God for different results.

A stronghold in the mind is not just a bad habit; it is a settled way of seeing that resists God's perspective. It can be a belief about yourself, like "I'll never change," or a belief about God, like "He doesn't really come through for me." These thoughts feel normal because we have rehearsed them for years, sometimes since childhood. But when the Word of God shines light on those areas, it exposes them not to shame us but to invite us into freedom. Light always gives us a choice: cling to the familiar lie, or step into the unfamiliar truth. Honestly, that can feel uncomfortable. Sometimes we would rather stay with what we know, even if it keeps us stuck.

The renewed mind is built through repeated encounters with truth. Not just reading words on a page but allowing the Holy Spirit to make those words alive and personal. As we meditate on Scripture, speak it, pray it, and act on it, new pathways form in our thinking. Over time, what once felt impossible starts to feel normal. Forgiveness becomes less like a heroic act and more like a natural response. Trusting God in uncertainty stops feeling reckless and starts feeling right. This doesn't mean we never feel fear or confusion; it means those feelings no longer get the final say.

There is also a humility that comes with a renewed mind. We begin to realize how limited our understanding has been and how much we need the Spirit to teach us. Instead of leaning solely on our own reasoning, we become quicker to ask, "Lord, what are You saying about this?" That simple shift opens the door for divine insight in everyday situations—decisions about relationships, work, ministry, and even how we respond to conflict. The renewed mind creates space for heaven's wisdom to interrupt earth's noise.

Spiritual maturity is not measured only by how much Scripture we can quote, but by how deeply our thinking has been shaped by it. You can memorize verses and still panic at every problem if those verses have not penetrated your inner framework. But when truth sinks deep, it steadies you. Trials still hurt. Loss is still real. But underneath it all, there is an anchor—a quiet confidence that God is present and working even when you don't understand how. That confidence is a sign of a mind that is being renewed.

As renewal continues, our identity becomes more settled in what God says than in what we feel or what others say. We stop defining ourselves primarily by past failures, current struggles, or human labels. Instead, we start seeing ourselves as sons and daughters who carry His Spirit. That shift alone changes how we pray, how we resist temptation, and how we treat other people. When you see yourself as loved and chosen, obedience stops feeling like pressure and starts feeling like alignment with who you really are.

A renewed mind also changes how we see the impossible. Where the carnal mind says, "That could never happen," the renewed mind says, "If God said it, there is a way." It doesn't ignore facts, but it refuses to be imprisoned by them. It leaves room for miracles, for sudden turnarounds, for God to move outside the neat lines of our expectations. This kind of thinking is not fantasy; it is faith agreeing with the character and power of God.

This is especially important in unstable times. When the world feels like it's shaking—economically, politically, socially—the unrenewed mind absorbs that instability and lives in constant anxiety. But the renewed mind remembers that we belong to an unshakable Kingdom. That doesn't make us passive or careless; it makes us steady. We can engage with the world's problems without being swallowed by them because our inner world is anchored somewhere higher.

Mind renewal is not a one-time event at salvation; it is an ongoing process. There will be days when old thought patterns try to resurface, when fear feels louder than faith, when circumstances seem to contradict everything you believe. In those moments, renewal looks like returning to truth again. Speaking it even when you don't feel it. Choosing to believe God's Word over your emotions. Little by little, those choices reshape the inner landscape of your life.

Eventually, the renewed mind becomes a place where the Spirit feels at home. Instead of constant inner conflict, there is increasing agreement between what God is saying in your spirit and what you are thinking in your mind. That harmony is powerful. It positions you to walk in discernment, to recognize God's leading more easily, and to respond with obedience instead of hesitation. The more the mind is renewed, the more naturally the life of the Spirit flows through you into everyday situations.

And this is where the inheritance mentioned earlier starts becoming visible. Peace that doesn't make sense. Joy in hard seasons. Wisdom beyond your experience. Authority in prayer. Love for people you once found difficult. These are not personality upgrades; they are signs of Christ's life expressing itself through a mind that has been renewed. The supernatural life stops being a general idea and starts showing up in very practical ways.

So the call to renew the mind is really a call to step into what has already been given. It is an invitation to let light keep entering until there are fewer and fewer shadowed corners where old lies can hide. It is the daily decision to value God's perspective above our own, even when we don't fully understand it yet. As that happens, strongholds fall, truth takes root, and we begin to live not just as people who believe in the Spirit, but as people who truly walk in Him.

Casting the devil out is the easiest part of deliverance ministry. The most difficult part is destroying the mental strongholds in the minds of people that satan began to build in us from childhood. The real challenge is dismantling the spiritual structures of satan in our minds that entered as sciences and philosophies. These things condition believers to live as fallen men and disconnect us from what's available now through the cross and resurrection.

For this reason, don't think that all you need is someone to lay hands on you. Though powerful, it only complements the function of revelation in the life of the believer. This is why so many believers who don't value teaching run from place to place for hands to be laid on them, but in all their efforts, impartations, and fire tunnels, they still fall short of the transformation they deeply desire.

The issue is not the laying on of hands. The issue is thinking it's all you need. You fell under the power, but you got up still thinking like an atheist. You were laid out on the floor, but you still hold your reasoning and intellect as the be-all and end-all. This is why God wants to flood us with light. He desires to destroy these dark demonic structures by exposing us to His glory and knowledge. An ignorant believer agrees with the devil far more than we realize.

In the same way that we submit to the teaching of this natural world, we must learn about the things of the Spirit. This is one of the reasons that it matters what church you go to. Who you learn from matters, and what voices influence you matter. Now, to really understand why mind renewal is so central, we must talk more deeply about strongholds and the different conditions of the mind described in Scripture.

A stronghold is a fortified pattern of thinking that has been built over time through repeated thoughts, experiences, teachings, trauma, or lies. It is not just a passing thought; it is a mental structure. It becomes the grid through which we interpret reality. Strongholds often form early in life—through rejection, failure, abuse, fear, religion without revelation, or cultural beliefs that contradict God's truth.

For example, if a child grows up constantly criticized, a stronghold of "I am not good enough" can form. That belief then filters everything—relationships, calling, even how they see God. When they read Scripture about being loved and chosen, it clashes with the stronghold. Instead of receiving truth easily, they struggle to believe it. That is what a stronghold does: it resists God's perspective and defends a lie as if it were truth.

Paul talks about "*...arguments and every high thing that exalts itself against the knowledge of God*" (2 Corinthians 10:5 NKJV). That is stronghold language. These are mental arguments that contradict what God has revealed. They may sound intelligent, logical, or even humble, but if they disagree with God's Word, they are fortresses of deception.

This is why the battle for transformation is so focused on the mind. Even after someone is born again, their spirit is made new instantly, but their mind still carries old patterns.

The unrenewed mind defaults to survival, fear, self-protection, pride, shame, and natural reasoning. It interprets life through past wounds instead of present truth.

Scripture speaks about "*...the spirit of your mind...*" (Ephesians 4:23 NKJV). That phrase points to the inner atmosphere or governing influence behind our thoughts. Your mind is not just a neutral processor of information. It has a "spirit"—a bent, a tone, a direction. Before Christ, the spirit of our mind was shaped by the world, the flesh, and the enemy. After salvation, the Holy Spirit begins to reshape that inner atmosphere so our thinking aligns with heaven.

SEVERAL CONDITIONS OF THE MIND

- **The Carnal Mind:** This is the mind ruled by the senses and natural reasoning. It may be educated, disciplined, and moral, but it does not submit to God's truth when it contradicts human logic. It is uncomfortable with the supernatural and often explains away what it cannot control.
- **The Darkened Mind:** Scripture also speaks of minds that are darkened in understanding. This happens when people consistently reject the truth. Darkness is not just ignorance; it is resistance to light. Over time, a person can become numb to spiritual reality.
- **The Double Mind:** A divided mind tries to agree with God and the world at the same time. One moment it believes; the next it doubts. This instability makes it hard to walk in consistent faith because the inner foundation is split.
- **The Renewing Mind:** This is the mind in process. It still faces old thoughts, but it is actively being reshaped by

truth. It is learning to pause, to question old assumptions, and to bring thoughts into alignment with Christ.
- **The Renewed Mind**: This is the mind that has been so saturated with truth that agreement with God becomes the default. It is not perfect, but it is stable, spiritually aware, and quick to respond to the Spirit.

Mind renewal, then, is the lifelong process of tearing down strongholds and rebuilding according to truth. It happens through teaching, meditation on Scripture, obedience, and the work of the Holy Spirit. As these old mental structures fall, the life of the Spirit flows more freely. The believer begins to think with the mind of Christ, respond with the heart of Christ, and walk in the freedom that was theirs all along.

You see, the mind is very powerful. This is one of the reasons why God wants to transform our minds. Things like doubt and unbelief, which are hindrances to the supernatural and to God intervening in our affairs, are made from thoughts and from the character of our mindset. I remember years ago, after being born again, I still struggled in life. I had no victory. It seemed in many ways that my life got worse. If I were looking at things from a natural perspective, it felt like every day was full of struggle. Every day seemed like a battle. I seemed to be in constant need of deliverance. And while it is true that I did need deliverance from certain things and I was, and still am, going through the process of sanctification. The greatest need I had—without realizing it—was a renewed mind.

The Bible says, "*For as he thinks in his heart, so is he*" (Proverbs 23:7 NKJV). In the spirit, your life can only become what your heart meditates on. God's desire is to so transform your heart and align it with Him that you can become who He designed and called you to be. Our thoughts are actually very powerful and creative in nature. This is why God told Joshua, *"This Book of the Law shall not depart from your mouth, but you shall meditate in it day and night...then you will have good success"* (Joshua 1:8 NKJV).

Notice that his success was not only connected to what he said, but also to his meditation. You believe whatever you meditate on, and there's a relationship between your belief and your words. That's why the Bible says, *"I believed, therefore have I spoken..."* (Psalm 116:10 KJV). So for God to change your speaking, He has to change your heart.

In Proverbs 4:23 (NKJV), the Bible says to *"keep your heart with all diligence, for out of it springs the issues of life."* In other words, many issues in life gain authority because they are spoken, and many problems actually begin in the heart, a term often used interchangeably with the spirit or the mind. There was a major key that God shared with me as it relates to receiving from Him. When the woman with the issue of blood had an opportunity to touch the hem of Jesus' garment to be healed, she did not pass up the moment. There was a crowd of people thronging Jesus. It puts you in the mind of a celebrity walking through a crowd and how desperate people would be to touch their shoulder or arm, or to get the attention of their favorite celebrity. But all of their thronging did not get Jesus' attention. There was a special touch where virtue came out of Him.

In other words, not only did she touch Him physically, but she withdrew from what was in His spirit. Think of this like religious activity with no breakthrough, prayer with no answers, worship with no manifestation of His presence. All of these describe actions similar to people touching Jesus. But what made the woman with the issue of blood different was her faith—and this began with a thought. The Bible says she said within herself, *If I can just touch the hem of His garment, I will be healed.* This thought defined what she wanted and what she needed. There was unity between her belief and her actions, and this brought manifestation. In her mind, it was settled. That is what made her touch different.

We can speak about something but not believe it. Many times, our inward conversation reveals whether we are in faith or in doubt. But the great news is that belief is simply a choice. We have the authority to choose to believe. After suffering through many situations and even times where I felt like God had forgotten about me, I began to learn to meditate on the Word of God and to see myself and my life as a manifestation of the Word of God—even when I wasn't there yet, even when it didn't seem true. I began to meditate on it anyway.

We must renounce the lies of the devil. We have to resist him with the Word of God. We have to cast down every imagination and every high thing that exalts itself above the knowledge of God. Satan wants you to meditate on his lies because if this becomes the character of your thought life, those lies will manifest in your life, become part of your speech, and bring death, curses, and misfortune into your life. But when the mind is renewed, when God speaks to your spirit, your mind won't resist what God is revealing.

Even in Scripture, where the Bible says that God is "*...able to do exceedingly abundantly above all that we ask or think, according to the power that works in us*" (Ephesians 3:20 NKJV), there is a powerful truth: God reveals two dimensions that activate the power—asking and thinking. That means in the mind of God, our thinking can actually be a form of prayer. In the days of Noah, the Bible describes a time when men's imaginations were continually evil, and their imagination was so important to God that it was one of the reasons He sent the flood. If imagination were useless, why would God mention it?

Even in Matthew 5, the Bible tells us that if we lust after a woman, the thought is treated like the action. That's because thoughts are the place of origin. Whatever a person does reflects what was first in their mind, whether good or bad. So when God wants to transform a person's life, He puts His Word in their spirit and gives them understanding. What starts in the spirit gets into the mind, and from the inward man, transformation begins to happen. When you think supernaturally, supernatural things happen.

ACTIVATION

Father, I thank You for destroying every stronghold in my mind. I thank You for filling me with the intimate knowledge of Jesus. I thank You right now, God, for giving me the fear of the Lord so that You can begin to give me wisdom and knowledge. Right now, Lord, I repent for any ignorance I've had about Your Kingdom. I repent of the carnal mind and carnal thinking. I will no longer be ruled by my senses, but I will walk by faith and live by faith. I thank You, God, for renewing my mind and giving me spiritual knowledge so that I can partner with You and see things from Your heavenly perspective. I pray right now, God, that You show me Your ways. In Jesus' name. Amen.

CHAPTER 6

MOUNTAIN-MOVING FAITH

Without faith, it is impossible to please God. One of the most vital aspects of being born again is faith, and as sons, we must grow into maturity in it. We must understand faith, because we are called to live by it. When a believer lacks understanding of faith, they not only struggle to please God, but they also find it difficult to access what Christ has already made available. Where there is no faith, God can do nothing.

The clearest and most powerful definition of faith is found in Hebrews 11:1 (KJV): *"Now faith is the substance of things hoped for, the evidence of things not seen."* When we take a closer look at this verse, we see that faith is described as a substance—something real, yet invisible. Simply put, faith is an actual existing reality, but one that exists in the spirit realm. While it is true that you are spirit, you still live in the natural world; therefore, faith enables you to operate according to supernatural laws while still on earth.

When a person first becomes born again, they must confess with their mouth that they believe Jesus died for our sins, went to hell, and rose again on the third day. Then they declare Him as Lord. The fact that salvation begins this way is extremely powerful. A person cannot be born again without believing in the resurrection of Christ. When we consider how death is viewed, it becomes clear that it is regarded as the most final and unchangeable circumstance. When someone dies, people grieve and offer condolences because death appears irreversible.

Now consider this: your faith begins with believing in Christ's resurrection from the dead. By His wisdom, God chose to begin your faith journey with the overcoming of the most impossible condition—death itself. In other words, if you believe in resurrection from the dead, there is nothing else beyond your ability to believe. God established your faith from that starting point. As a believer, it is a lie to say you do not have faith for financial miracles or for mountains to move. The faith within you is powerful—it is the same faith the Father used to raise Christ from the dead.

In Scripture, Jesus tells His disciples that if they had faith as small as a mustard seed, they could move mountains. This verse is often misinterpreted. Many believers spend their lives searching for more faith, feeling as though they do not have enough for what they are facing. As a result, they fail to exercise the authority God has already given them. What Jesus is revealing here is life-altering if truly understood.

The disciples had just failed to cast an evil spirit out of a boy. Jesus, having come down from prayer, easily cast the spirit out. Later, the disciples asked Him why they were unable to do it. Jesus told them it was because of their unbelief. He then spoke about mustard-seed faith being able to move mountains. Notice that Jesus never told them their faith needed to increase. Instead, He was shifting their understanding—helping them realize the power of the faith they already possessed. The issue was not a lack of faith, but unbelief.

This raises an important question: could the unbelief many believers struggle with be rooted in not believing in what they already have from God? This is why Jesus emphasized how much power even a very small amount of faith carries. We must recognize that we already possess the faith of God within us.

In Mark 11:22 (NKJV), Jesus instructed His disciples to *"Have faith in God."* It is important to remember that they were living under the old covenant at that time. They did not yet have the new covenant with its better promises. The faith Jesus spoke of then is now already present in every born-again believer. Everything about God and His nature has been imparted into your spirit. This is why Scripture tells us that Jesus is the vine and we are the branches.

Jesus explains that the God-kind of life flows from the vine into the branches. There is no difference between life in the branch and life in the vine. Because of this shared life, the branch produces fruit—the same fruit Jesus Himself would produce. The Bible says, *"If you abide in Me, and My words abide in you, you will ask what you desire, and it shall be done for you"* (John 15:7 NKJV). Here, Jesus is describing His own nature—His life, His authority, and His faith—being active in you because of your new life in Him. You may be asking, "If I have the God-kind of faith, why doesn't it always feel like it?" The answer is the unrenewed mind. Any area in which we are ignorant of the Word of God is an area where the mind has not yet been renewed. Scripture refers to this as the carnal mind.

In Romans, we are told that to be carnally minded is death, but to be spiritually minded is life and peace. This means our thinking determines whether we live in the realm of life and peace or experience the realm of death. In the realm of death, finances, relationships, marriages, and even physical health deteriorate. When we repent—meaning we change our mind—God is inviting us out of death and into life. This is why we do not want to think carnally; we desire life and peace.

A carnal person does not live by faith. Therefore, we must understand what carnality truly is. Scripturally, believers generally fall into two categories: the learned and the unlearned. The unlearned are often described as carnal. The word *carnal*, translated from the Greek, simply means "flesh" or "of the flesh." It refers to someone governed primarily by natural reasoning or human impulses rather than by the Spirit of God.

Unfortunately, this term is frequently misunderstood. Many assume that a "carnal Christian" is morally corrupt or intentionally sinful. However, carnality in the biblical sense is not primarily about outward behavior; it is about spiritual maturity and one's way of thinking. When a believer does not yet understand or yield to the Spirit-life, the only way they can function is from the natural mind.

To be carnal, then, is to operate predominantly from human reasoning rather than spiritual understanding. It does not mean a person lacks genuine faith; it means their discernment is still shaped by the natural realm instead of the Spirit. Their spirit has been made new, but their mind has not yet caught up with that reality.

Thus, carnality is not a condemnation of a believer's character, but an indication of undeveloped spiritual understanding—a call to grow, renew the mind, and learn to live from the life of the Spirit. The more renewed the mind is, the less arguments, reasonings, ideologies, and ways of thinking called strongholds can stop you from thinking as God does, which causes you to be more likely to speak as he would speak. One of the first things that must happen for you to truly grow is exercising the faith that is in you. Every reference to little faith in scripture is when faith was not exercised.

SPEAKING

When it comes to faith, speaking is not optional—it is central to its operation. Faith is not merely something we hold internally; it is something that must be released outwardly through words. Scripture consistently reveals that the movement of God's power from the invisible realm into the natural world happens through speech.

Hebrews 11 frames faith by showing us that there are two realms: the unseen and the seen. It teaches that what is visible was made from what is invisible. Faith, then, begins with an awareness of the unseen reality, a confidence that it exists, and a conviction that it governs what we experience in the natural world. Crucially, both realms were created the same way—by speaking. God spoke, and the unseen came into being. God spoke again, and the unseen manifested. Words are the bridge between worlds. This pattern is not limited to creation—it continues throughout Scripture.

Jesus demonstrated this vividly when He spoke to the fig tree. He did not speak about it or around it; He spoke to it. The tree heard Him, responded, and withered. This was not symbolic language—it was a demonstration of authority. The fig tree responded because it was created by words and remains subject to words. Jesus was not doing something new; He was operating according to the original design of creation.

The same principle is seen in God's instruction to Moses at the rock. God commanded Moses to speak to the rock so that water would flow. The instruction itself reveals something profound: the rock had the capacity to hear. Creation responds to speech because it was formed by speech. Moses' failure was not simply disobedience—it was a failure to honor the power of words in God's system.

Earlier, Moses also spoke to the earth. In response, the ground opened and swallowed those in rebellion. Again, the earth heard and obeyed. The natural world is not deaf—it is attentive to the authority embedded in God's words and in words spoken under His authority.

Joshua provides another striking example when he spoke to the sun and the moon. He commanded them to stand still, and they obeyed. Time itself paused because Joshua spoke. This event underscores a truth we often overlook: the sun, the moon, and the cosmos were all created by the word of God, and they remain responsive to spoken authority aligned with His will. These examples are not isolated miracles; they are revelations of how reality functions. Everything God created has the capacity to hear, because everything was created by hearing God speak.

This is why Jesus' teaching about the vine and the branches is so significant. He tells His disciples to abide in Him and to let His word abide in them. The result of that abiding is not silence—it is speech. When His word lives in us, we are empowered to speak in alignment with Him. Faith gives us the ability to speak with delegated authority, not as independent creators, but as vessels through which God's word flows.

If you are going to live by faith, you must understand that the natural world you inhabit must be spoken to. Silence does not move mountains; words do. Faith is released through speaking, and speaking brings manifestation. Your words—when aligned with God's word—become the means by which the supernatural enters the natural.

The unseen realm responds to faith, and the seen realm responds to words. This is how God designed reality to function. Faith connects you to heaven, but words exercise authority on the earth. From the beginning, creation itself was framed by spoken command—God said, and what was invisible became visible. Humanity, made in His image, was entrusted with dominion, and dominion is largely exercised through speech. For this reason, there should not be a single domain of your life that you do not speak to. Your world is continually being shaped, ordered, or resisted by the words you release.

This principle is powerfully illustrated in the life of Job. Scripture describes Job as blameless and upright, and it explicitly tells us that God placed a hedge of protection around him. When satan appears before God, he acknowledges that hedge and admits he cannot touch Job without permission. In the first encounter, satan is allowed access to Job's possessions and family. In the second, he is permitted to afflict Job's body. In both conversations, God draws a firm boundary: Job's life is not to be taken. Satan is given access, but not authority over death.

Immediately after this second trial begins, Job's wife urges him to "curse God and die." This is not accidental. If satan already had authority to kill Job, there would be no reason to provoke Job's speech. Satan understood that authority on earth operates through human agreement, and that words are how agreement is established. Though God had forbidden Job's death, if Job had spoken death himself—if he had aligned his words with the accuser—he would have opened a legal door in the earthly realm. This reveals the weight God has placed on human speech. Heaven sets limits, but the earth responds to words.

That same truth appears in the account of Jesus and Peter paying the temple tax recorded in the Gospel of Matthew. This detail matters because the temple tax was not a Roman civil tax. It originated in the Law of Moses as a half-shekel offering required of every adult Jewish male for the upkeep of the temple. It was a covenantal tax—tied to worship, identity, and participation in God's house. By the time of Jesus, it had become a symbol of religious obligation and social pressure. The collectors confront Peter, not to ask politely, but to test whether Jesus considers Himself obligated to the system. Peter instinctively answers yes and then goes to Jesus for clarity.

Jesus responds by teaching something profound before ever solving the financial problem. He explains that kings do not tax their own sons. In other words, as the Son of God, He is not actually obligated to pay this tax at all. This establishes an important spiritual truth: Jesus is operating from sonship, not servitude. Yet He immediately adds that they will pay the tax anyway, "lest we cause offense." This shows that freedom does not remove responsibility, and authority does not require rebellion. Jesus chooses peace without surrendering identity.

Then comes the method. Jesus does not tell Peter to borrow money, work harder, or appeal to others. He gives a word. "Go to the sea, cast a hook, take the first fish you catch, and you will find a coin in its mouth." This instruction is layered with meaning. In Scripture, water frequently represents multitudes of people, nations, or systems. Fish consistently represent people, especially in the language Jesus used when He called His disciples fishers of men. The coin was not lying on the shore or falling from the sky—it was already present, hidden, carried within the system. The provision existed, but it was accessed through obedience to a spoken word.

The detail that the coin was in the mouth of the fish is especially important. Mouths release words. Provision came from the mouth. The implication is not subtle: solutions move through speech. Jesus did not speak directly to the tax collectors or to the temple system—He spoke to Peter, and Peter acted on the word. The miracle began the moment Jesus spoke, not the moment Peter caught the fish. This teaches that provision is often waiting within systems and people, but it is unlocked by words aligned with heaven.

This account shows that even financial matters respond to spiritual authority exercised through speech. Jesus demonstrated that He was not subject to the system, yet He could command provision from within it. That same principle applies to believers. Your words do not merely describe your circumstances; they engage them. They either authorize resistance or release supply. Words set things in motion. They can dispatch angels or empower demons. They can give authority to sickness or to healing, to lack or to abundance. God has designed reality so that faith connects you to the unseen, but words govern what manifests in the seen.

And this is where we have to slow down and be really honest, because most believers agree with this in theory, but we don't always live as we believe it. I'm including myself in that, because there are times I've caught myself talking like a person who has no covenant, no authority, and no hope. Like I'll read one scripture about God supplying all my needs, and then five minutes later I'm telling someone, "Man, I don't know how I'm gonna make it." That's not just "being real," that's two kingdoms fighting for the microphone. And the hard part is that the second voice often sounds more reasonable. It sounds responsible. It sounds like "wisdom." But faith doesn't ignore wisdom; it just refuses to bow to fear dressed up as logic.

If words are the bridge between realms, then unbelief is often the demolition crew. And unbelief isn't always this dramatic thing where someone shakes their fist at God and says, "I don't believe!" Unbelief is usually subtle. It's the quiet inner conclusion that God won't do what He said, or that He might do it for someone else but not for you, or that this situation is different because it's "too far gone." Unbelief is when you mentally agree that resurrection is true as a doctrine, but you don't let resurrection thinking touch your marriage, your finances, your mind, your body, or your future.

That's why I said earlier the issue was not a lack of faith but unbelief, and that's exactly right. Faith can be present, and unbelief can still be active. It's like having a seed in the ground but pouring salt over the soil every day. The seed is real. Life is in it. But something is continually resisting its growth. This is why Jesus could look at disciples who left everything to follow Him and still say, "O you of little faith." It wasn't an insult; it was a diagnosis. He wasn't saying they had none. He was saying they had not been using it when it mattered.

And I think sometimes believers get stuck because they treat faith like a feeling instead of a substance. If faith is "substance," then it is not the same as emotion. You can feel afraid and still have faith. You can feel tired and still have faith. You can feel discouraged and still have faith. Faith doesn't always feel like fireworks. A lot of times, faith feels like you're standing there with nothing but a word from God, and you're deciding, again and again, that His word is more solid than what your eyes are reporting.

Hearing "Where there is no faith, God can do nothing" is something that people might bristle at, retorting, "God can do anything!" And yes, God is Almighty, but He has chosen to work through covenant order. He has chosen to partner with people. The Bible repeatedly shows that unbelief limits what God does in a region or a moment. Not because God is weak, but because He honors the way He designed relationship. He doesn't bulldoze human will. Faith is the place where our will agrees with His will. And agreement is powerful. That's why Jesus could say, *"According to your faith be it unto you"* (Matthew 9:29 KJV). That statement alone tells you faith is not decorative. It's not a religious accessory. It is how spiritual supply is received.

So if we're going to talk about faith as sons growing into maturity, we must talk about responsibility. Not condemnation, but responsibility. Sons don't just talk about inheritance; they learn how to steward it. Babies cry for what they want. Sons learn how the house works. Sons learn how their father does things. Sons carry the father's nature and represent the father's authority. And that's why this matters: faith is not merely how you get things from God. Faith is how you learn to function like family.

This is also why the connection between faith and the renewed mind is so important. The unrenewed mind will sabotage faith even while the spirit is alive. The spirit is made new, but the mind hasn't caught up yet. That means you can genuinely be born again and still think like an orphan. You can pray like an orphan, interpret God as an orphan, hear a promise, and immediately add ten "Yeah, but" rebuttals—that's orphan thinking. And it doesn't mean you aren't saved; it means your mind hasn't been renewed.

Romans says, *"For to be carnally minded is death..."* (Romans 8:6 NKJV). That verse is heavy because it means death is not only an event; it can be an atmosphere. It can be a realm you function in. It can be the tone of your life. Death shows up as dread, decay, hopelessness, constant breakdown, things wearing out, relationships draining, health deteriorating, and joy disappearing. And notice it doesn't say carnally minded is "bad." It says it is death. Meaning, it produces death. It releases death. It agrees with the curse without even realizing it.

But to be spiritually minded is life and peace. I love that it doesn't just say life; it says life and peace. Because peace is one of the greatest signs you're thinking from the Spirit. Peace doesn't mean there's no battle. Peace means the battle isn't living inside you. Peace means you can be surrounded by pressure and still have an inner steadiness that doesn't make sense to a carnal mind. That's why peace is supernatural. Real peace is not personality. It's a fruit. It is evidence of another realm.

Understanding that believers can be "learned" or "unlearned" is so important, and honestly, it's where a lot of people get offended. They think "learned" means educated in the world's system. But in Scripture, being learned is being taught by God. It's being trained in spiritual reality. It is learning the ways of the Kingdom. And being "unlearned" is not an insult either. It is simply describing someone who hasn't been discipled in the realm of the Spirit. Many people have been in church for years and remain unlearned spiritually because they've been entertained, not trained. They've been comforted, not equipped. They've been given sermons but not understanding. And where understanding is missing, ignorance remains—ignorance is not neutral.

This is why the Holy Spirit is called Teacher. He doesn't just comfort; He teaches. He brings remembrance. He guides into all truth. And truth is what renews the mind, and a renewed mind activates the faith you possess, allowing it to manifest in your life.

Now, let's deal with this idea of "little faith" again, because this is important to understand. Every reference to little faith is when faith was not exercised. That's key. Jesus never scolded people for having little faith when they were actively stepping out. He corrected little faith when they panicked, when they doubted, when they stopped using what they had. So little faith isn't about quantity, it's about function. It's like having muscles but never lifting anything. The muscles are there, but they remain weak because they're not being used. Faith grows stronger through use, not through wishing. And you don't use faith primarily by a feeling of intensity. You use it by acting on the Word and speaking in agreement with it.

Which brings us back to speaking again, and honestly, speaking is where a lot of believers either mature fast or stay stuck for years. Because it's one thing to believe quietly in your heart, and it's another thing to let your mouth come under the government of heaven. The mouth is not just a communication tool. Biblically, the mouth is a steering wheel. James says the tongue is like a rudder on a ship. The rudder is small, but it determines direction. This means you can be praying for God to "take you somewhere," but your tongue is steering you somewhere else. And sometimes we're asking God to override our speech while we keep blessing fear, blessing lack, blessing sickness, and blessing failure with our words.

And I know people don't like hearing that because it feels like pressure. But it's not pressure if you understand it as identity. This is not "try harder to say the right thing." This is "come into alignment with what is already true about who you are." You're not a powerless person begging for crumbs. You're a branch connected to the Vine. His life flows into you. And His words are meant to abide in you. If His words abide in you, they don't just sit in your head; they come out of your mouth.

That's why the "abide in me" passage is so intense. *"If ye abide in me, and my words abide in you, ye shall ask what ye will, and it shall be done..."* (John 15:7 KJV). That isn't a blank check for selfishness. It's describing what happens when your will gets saturated by His word. You're asking for changes. Your speaking changes. You stop speaking from anxiety, and you start speaking from union.

UNION CHANGES VOCABULARY

It is important to understand how speaking works with faith. Consider that creation was framed by words, which is confirmed by the writer of Hebrews by indicating the worlds were framed by the word of God, so that things seen were made from things unseen. "Framed" is interesting because it implies structure. Order. Boundaries. Like the framework of a house. The unseen realm is not random spiritual fog. It is structured. It has laws. And faith is how we access those laws. Then words are how we enforce them in the natural realm.

That's why Jesus didn't just "believe" the fig tree would wither. He spoke. And He didn't speak politely either. He cursed it. Which means He judged it. He rendered a verdict in the Spirit and then released it through words. The disciples were shocked, not because the tree withered, but because it obeyed so fast. And Jesus responded like, "Yeah...have faith in God." Meaning, this is a normal Kingdom function if you understand it.

The same thing happens with mountains. Jesus didn't say, "If you have faith, you can ask God to move mountains." He said the person who has faith says to the mountain, *"Be removed..."* (Matthew 21:21 NKJV). That means faith doesn't only pray; faith speaks to obstacles. Faith does pray, yes, but faith also commands when God has given authority. And the reason so many Christians don't do that is that they don't know what belongs to them, and they're afraid of being disappointed. So they stay "safe" and only pray vague prayers. But authority is not vague. Authority is specific. Authority speaks directly.

Now, when you talk about Moses being told to speak to the rock, that's a massive example. God wanted Moses to represent Him accurately. God's system is not rage-driven. Moses struck the rock in frustration, and God treated it seriously. Not because God was petty, but because Moses was modeling God to a nation. He was showing them how God functions.

And God wanted them to learn provision flows through spoken authority, not through carnal anger. The rock hearing Moses isn't weird if you accept creation as responsive. It's only weird if you assume the natural realm is disconnected from spiritual law. But it's not. It's held together by the word of God.

Joshua speaking to the sun and moon is also wild, and people try to explain it away because it messes with natural law. But that's the point. The supernatural overrides natural order when God is involved. Faith is not limited by physics. Physics describes the consistent behavior of the natural realm. But the supernatural is not the natural realm behaving consistently; it is a higher order intervening. So when Joshua spoke, he wasn't doing a science experiment. He was exercising authority in alignment with God's will in a moment of covenant warfare. And creation responded.

It makes sense that everything God created has the capacity to hear—it's spiritual mechanics. If God made everything by speaking, then everything was made by hearing. So creation is hearing-based. That includes your body. That includes systems. That includes atmospheres. That includes your own soul.

Your own heart hears you. Your mind hears you. Your emotions hear you. That's why words can either strengthen faith or strengthen fear. You can literally train your inner world by what you allow yourself to keep saying.

The example of Job is important because it shows something many people overlook: satan wanted agreement. He wanted Job's mouth. Because accusation always wants a partnership. The enemy doesn't just want to attack you; he wants you to interpret the attack wrongly and then speak in agreement with it. "God left me." "This will never change." "I'm cursed." "I always lose." Those are not harmless venting statements. They are agreements. And agreement carries authority.

The wife saying "curse God and die" wasn't random. It was an invitation to come into agreement with death. Satan couldn't cross God's boundary directly. So he tried to get Job to cross it with his own mouth. That's huge. It means sometimes the enemy's strategy is not just to bring pressure, but to provoke speech. He wants you to say the thing that unlocks the door.

This is why it matters what we say in pain. Pain makes you talk. It just does. People talk when they're scared. People talk when they're angry. People talk when they're tired. And the enemy loves those moments because the tongue gets loose. But maturity is when you learn to suffer without surrendering your mouth.

And let's be realistic: we don't always do that perfectly. Sometimes we blow it. Sometimes we say dumb stuff. Sometimes we speak fear, and then later we're like, "Why did I even say that?" That's part of growth. The point is not perfection overnight. The point is increasing alignment. A renewed mind produces a governed mouth over time.

It is significant to note that in the account of the temple tax mentioned in Matthew 17:24–27, the specific portion required was pulled directly from the mouth of a fish. While many overlook this detail, the essence of the miracle was found in the mouth. And the mouth represents speech. Provision came through the mouth. It's like God is constantly reinforcing the same principle: words matter, words carry weight, words release reality.

Also, Jesus' explanation about sons not being taxed is such a clear revelation of identity. He was basically telling Peter, "We don't pay because we're obligated; we pay because we're free." That's a different posture. And I think a lot of believers are trying to operate in faith while still thinking like servants. Servants do things to avoid punishment. Sons act from their rightful standing in relationship with their father. Servants think God is always irritated. Sons know the father is good. Servants beg. Sons ask. Servants hope, maybe. Sons expect because they know the nature of the house.

When addressing faith and maturity as sons, the focus is truly on learning the language of the Household of God. In every healthy house, the kids learn what their father is like. They learn what they can ask for. They learn what the father says yes to. They learn what is out of bounds. They learn where the fridge is. They learn that they belong. It's normal. Spiritual maturity is similar. Faith is learning what kind of Father God is and then speaking and acting as you believe it.

Here's another piece we should add. Faith is not only a tool for obtaining things, but it is a posture of the heart that honors God. Faith says God is truthful. Faith says God is capable. Faith says God is consistent. That's why it pleases Him. It's not that God is impressed by our confidence like we're doing a performance. It's that faith agrees with His character. Unbelief calls God a liar, even if we don't mean to. And that's why unbelief is serious. It's not just "doubt," it's an accusation against the nature of God.

But again, we need to be careful: people can struggle with doubt and still be sincerely pursuing God. The goal is not to shame doubters. The goal is to teach believers how to move from doubt to faith. And that road is usually built with truth, repetition, and practice. It's built with testimonies, with the Word, with seeing God come through, with being stretched, and sometimes with failing and learning and coming back again.

That's why the renewed mind is so essential. Your spirit may have the faith of God in it, but your mind can argue with it all day. Your mind can pull up every past disappointment, every unanswered prayer, every story of "it didn't work," and it will try to use that as evidence against God's Word. But Hebrews says faith is the evidence of things not seen. Which means faith doesn't use visible circumstances as its primary evidence. Faith uses God's Word as evidence. That's why faith comes by hearing, and hearing by the Word of God. Hearing is how faith is activated. Not just hearing sound waves but hearing revelation. Hearing truth until it becomes more real than what you see.

And honestly, this is where people quit too early. They hear the Word, they get excited, they try one time, then something goes wrong, and they decide it "doesn't work." But faith is not a slot machine. It's relationship and law working together. Sometimes resistance shows up not because you're doing it wrong, but because you're doing it right and the enemy doesn't like it. Daniel prayed, and there was a delay, not because God didn't answer, but because there was warfare in the unseen. That's another reason speaking matters: persistence matters. If words are how we enforce the will of God in the earth, then consistent words matter. You don't speak once and then quit. You speak, and you keep speaking, because you are holding your ground until the seen realm aligns with what heaven has already spoken.

Now, all of this can sound intense, and I want to keep it human: there are seasons where it's hard to speak life. There are days when you feel like your words are hitting the ceiling and falling back down. There are moments when you don't feel "full of faith." But faith is not measured by how hyped you feel. Faith is measured by what you agree with when you don't feel hyped. Faith is what you return to when everything in you wants to panic.

And one of the biggest ways to grow is to start paying attention to the language you default to. What do you say when you're surprised? What do you say when you're under pressure? What do you say when you get a bad report? Because that's usually the raw material of what you truly believe, at least in that moment. And God isn't mad when we notice those things. He's inviting renewal. He's inviting repentance. Repentance is a change of mind, but it usually shows up first as a change of mouth.

So, practically, the mature son learns to speak to things, but he also learns when to speak and how to speak. He learns that complaining is not harmless. He learns that unbelief loves to hide inside "just being realistic." He learns that sarcasm can be a cloak for despair. He learns that words can partner with darkness even when the heart doesn't intend to. And he learns to bring his mouth back under the Lordship of Christ.

Because "Jesus is Lord" is not only a salvation statement. It's a daily statement. If He's Lord, then He's Lord over what I say. Lord over what I agree with. Lord over what I repeat. Lord over what I curse, what I bless, what I declare, what I tolerate.

And that brings us full circle: faith begins with resurrection. Which means the believer's entire life is supposed to be resurrection-shaped. Resurrection says, "This is not final." Resurrection says, "God can reverse what looks irreversible." Resurrection says, "Even if something dies, God can raise it." So when a believer says, "I don't have faith for that," what they're really saying is, "My mind hasn't been renewed to resurrection yet in that area." Because resurrection faith is already the starting point of salvation, that faith is in you.

So the journey is not "Lord give me faith." The journey is, "Lord, renew my mind until I actually live like what You already put in me is real." And then: "Lord, teach me to speak like a son." Because sons don't just survive, sons represent. Sons carry authority. Sons enforce the Kingdom within their sphere of influence. Sons speak to mountains and refuse to bow. Sons speak to storms and remember who is in the boat. Sons speak to lack and declare supply. Sons speak to sickness and command healing. Sons speak to their own souls and say, *"Why are you cast down...? Hope in God"* (Psalm 42:5 NKJV).

And sometimes, yeah, you might have to speak to yourself before you ever speak to the mountain because the first mountain is often the mind. The first storm is often internal. The first opposition is often the argument inside you that says, "This won't work." But when that argument gets confronted by truth, and when the mouth starts agreeing with heaven, strongholds start breaking. And you'll notice over time your faith stops being theoretical and becomes operational. It becomes a lifestyle—you stop visiting faith like a topic, and you start living by it like it's oxygen.

That's maturity. And it's not for "special believers." It's for sons. Faith is so powerful. In Dublin, California, I was ministering for my friends Sean Smith and Christa Smith at a Momentum Conference. Every day of the conference was so powerful, and the glory of God was building more and more. The last day of the conference was miracle night. I was asked to teach, demonstrate miracles and healing, and close the meetings.

When I began to speak, the atmosphere was charged with hunger, and I continued to speak words of faith by sharing testimonies. I shared miraculous stories I had experienced, and my words saturated an already presence-filled environment with faith. We can never reach the end of faith—there is always another realm.

Once the atmosphere was heavy with power, I began to call people up and lay hands on them. But I also spoke to diseases, cancers, blind eyes, deaf ears, scoliosis, arthritis, and many other infirmities. I view them all as mountains that need to move. Words of faith can create, and we saw many healings and creative miracles. We lost count as Jesus and His goodness was experienced, but it begins with our words.

What do you need to speak life to? What do you need to tell to move out of your way? It's time to speak to it.

ACTIVATION

Father, it's in Jesus' name. I thank You that I already have the faith of God. I already have the same life that is in Christ. I rebuke doubt and unbelief. I choose to agree with You right now, and I declare that every mountain of impossibility that stands in front of me is commanded to begin to move out of my way in the name of Jesus. I agree and declare that, right now, miracles are being released into my life. I declare right now that everything begins to turn in my favor, in Jesus' mighty name. I declare that this year is the year of deliverance and restoration of everything that has been lost in my life. I declare over every evil planting that the enemy has placed into my life—and every evil tree and fruit that has grown from it—I curse it and command it to die in the name of Jesus. And everything that has died in my life that I ever received from God, or that is supposed to belong to me, I command to come alive right now. I speak to the dry bones of my life, and I say, "Live again," in Jesus' mighty name.

CHAPTER 7
THE GRACE OF GOD

Today, many preach a grace of God that is divorced from the power of God, and as they begin to declare this grace, it distorts the true essence of what true grace really is. They claim that grace simply covers sin, and because we are under grace, there's no need to repent. This lie of hyper-grace is extremely dangerous and could cost many people their salvation but also cost them flowing in the power of God. In the context of this book, I want to make sure that it's understood that the grace of God empowers and has a relationship with power.

In the book of Acts, Jesus declares that when the Holy Spirit comes upon the disciples, they will begin to move in power. Acts 1:8 indicates it was His final conversation with them before He ascended to the Father. I want to note that usually, if someone is sharing first or last words, what they're stating holds more weight and significance than other things they say. It means these words are of the utmost importance. And it's interesting that Jesus' final conversation with the disciples was about authority and walking in power. This is something we cannot ignore, especially since our Lord Jesus placed emphasis on the empowerment that the Holy Spirit brings.

In another reference to this power, Jesus instructs the believers to "*...tarry in the city...until you are endued with power from on high*" (Luke 24:49 NKJV). He reinforces this in the Gospel of Mark, declaring that these signs will follow those who believe: "*In My name they will cast out demons; they will speak with new tongues... they will lay hands on the sick, and they will recover*" (Mark 16:17-18 NKJV). He further assures them that even if they drink anything deadly, it will by no means hurt them because of this divine power.

The final words of Jesus came to pass once they were filled with the Holy Spirit on the Day of Pentecost. And when this took place, they began to act in a way that mirrored drunken behavior, and so it wasn't understood what was happening, even as they spoke in divine tongues that had been imparted into their spirits. A crowd came because of the commotion, and once they arrived, they mocked it and said they were all just drunk. It's interesting that even in this generation, when the things of the Spirit are in operation, they are often met with mocking when people do not understand them.

Peter, being led by the Holy Spirit, lifted up his voice and began to give language to the experience that was taking place. He quoted the prophecy of Joel and said, "*...this is that which was spoken by the prophet Joel*" (Acts 2:16 KJV). He began to describe the Holy Spirit coming not just as in the past, where the Spirit was on some, where the Spirit would speak through some, where the Spirit would anoint some—but now the Holy Spirit was coming on all flesh, and they began to walk in the power of God.

But as we continue to read the book of Acts, we see a few things that are extremely thought-provoking. One of them is when we arrive in Acts chapter 5, and Ananias and Sapphira died because of lying to the Holy Spirit concerning money.

Once this took place, the fear of the Lord increased in the Church, and the direct result was that there was an increase of signs and wonders done by the hands of the apostles. I believe this is partially because the way they saw the apostles had changed. Ananias and Sapphira had lied directly to Peter, and this is why the Bible also says that in the height of the move of the Spirit, the people magnified the apostles. This was not in a negative light; it was in a posture of honor. You cannot receive from those you do not honor.

They were already moving in the power of the Spirit, but something shifted once the fear of the Lord increased in the Church. This is when, as Peter walked by, his shadow healed the sick. Over the years, I've heard many people preach about wanting their shadows to heal the sick, but I believe—as exemplified in scripture—a major key to seeing that type of spiritual reality or realm fall on a nation is to have the fear of the Lord and honor for who the Lord is using. Peter was neither praying nor prophesying when this happened. He was simply walking, but the hunger and faith of the people drew out of him the power of God that was inside him. And Scripture says that every person who came from the surrounding cities was healed. They entered a spiritual realm where 100 percent of the sick were completely healed. These were unprecedented times of God's power.

But I want to bring to your attention something so powerful in the Word of God. It says in Acts 4:33 (NKJV), "*And with great power the apostles gave witness of the resurrection of the Lord Jesus. And great grace was upon them all.*" It's interesting that in this passage, grace and power have a relationship. The increase of miracles, the increase of the supernatural, was in direct relationship with an increase in the grace of God. So from Acts chapter 1 to Acts chapter 5, we see ever-increasing glory. We see momentum. So to move in the power of God, we need the grace of God to increase upon our lives.

Paul said something so interesting about grace. He said that by the grace of God, he labored more than all the other apostles. The Scriptures also tell us that the grace of God is sufficient for us in the areas of our weakness. This means that the grace of God is divine empowerment. The powerful thing about grace is that whatever area you have grace in, you have God's very own ability.

Now, building on that foundation, we must clearly understand that grace is not passive permission—it is active participation in the life and power of God. Grace is not God lowering the standard; it is God supplying the strength to meet the standard through union with Christ. Hyper-grace teaching reduces grace to tolerance, but biblical grace releases transformation. True grace does not make sin safe; it makes holiness possible.

When grace is separated from power, Christianity becomes theoretical. You get forgiven people with no victory, saved people with no authority, and a church culture that talks about freedom but doesn't walk in it. But when grace and power flow together, you get believers who overcome sin, cast out devils, heal the sick, and live lives that look like Jesus. Grace is the pipeline through which heaven's ability flows into human weakness.

This is why Paul could say, *"But by the grace of God I am what I am..."* (1 Corinthians 15:10 NKJV) and then immediately talk about laboring more than the rest. Grace didn't make him passive—it made him effective. Grace didn't remove effort; it removed self-reliance. There is a huge difference. Human effort tries to produce spiritual results. Grace-empowered effort responds to what God is already supplying. One leads to burnout—the other leads to fruitfulness.

Grace also governs spiritual authority. You cannot operate in the power of God beyond the grace given to you. Grace is like a spiritual jurisdiction. Where grace rests, authority flows. This is why different believers carry different measures of impact—not because God plays favorites, but because grace grows where humility, faithfulness, and surrender grow. Scripture says God gives more grace to the humble. That means grace can increase. And where grace increases, power increases.

Notice again in Acts 4: great power, great grace. Not great talent. Not great charisma. Great grace. Grace was the invisible force behind visible miracles. The apostles were not superheroes; they were men carrying unusual measures of divine enablement. That same pattern continues today. If we want to see the power of God increase in our lives, we don't chase power—we posture ourselves for grace. We draw near to God, walk in humility, obey His voice, and stay dependent on Him. Grace rests on dependency, not self-confidence.

Grace is also what keeps power pure. Without grace, power can produce pride. But grace constantly reminds us that everything flowing through us is a gift, not a personal achievement. Grace keeps us low while God's power flows high. It protects the heart while expanding the ministry.

So grace is not the absence of standards. It is not an excuse to live casually. It is the very life of God working in us to do what we could never do on our own. Grace empowers repentance. Grace empowers obedience. Grace empowers boldness. Grace empowers endurance. Grace empowers miracles. Wherever grace is active, heaven's ability is present. And wherever heaven's ability is present, the power of God is never far behind.

ACTIVATION

Father, I thank You right now for Your grace. I pray wherever I'm weak, You increase Your grace in my life so I can be empowered to live as You lived. I pray right now, I receive all the grace I need to fulfill the calling in my destiny. I pray that it would be active in my life and increase right now in the name of Jesus. Lord, I repent for trying to do things in my own strength, and right now, God, I rest in the work You accomplished on the cross. Let Your grace be working in and through me so I can give You glory. Amen.

CHAPTER 8
SUPERNATURAL SECRETS

The fall of man was never about fruit. Fruit was just the conduit through which the real exchange occurred: sight for blindness, intimacy for independence, revelation for reasoning. The serpent didn't tempt Eve with rebellion; he tempted her with illumination. He suggested that God was withholding something essential, something necessary to become like Him: "Your eyes will be opened, and you will be like God." The tragedy is that they already were like Him. They were made in His image, carried His breath, walked in His authority, and lived in full awareness of His world. What they lost wasn't intelligence, but access. Not knowledge, but perception.

Scripture says that when they ate, their eyes were opened—but that opening wasn't an expansion. It was a collapse. It wasn't spiritual sight coming alive; it was spiritual sight going dark. Their awareness shifted from God to self, from spirit to flesh, from heaven to earth. For the first time, humanity became self-conscious apart from God. Shame entered not because their bodies changed, but because their vision did. The material world began to dominate the spirit-man, and the spirit that once perceived God's realm became muted. Adam and Eve didn't just break a rule; they lost a dimension.

That's why God's warning about death wasn't exaggerated. Death wasn't only physical—it was relational, functional, and spiritual. Sonship was fractured. Dominion was forfeited. The bloodline was corrupted. Access to the spirit realm was severed. Humanity didn't stop existing, but it stopped seeing. The devil targeted their sight because he understood something many believers still overlook: likeness to God isn't achieved by effort but rather by perception. To be like God, you must see like God.

From the beginning, humanity was designed to live by revelation. Adam's authority flowed from union with God. When God brought the animals to Adam to be named, He didn't coach him—He watched what Adam would call them. That shows us something powerful: Adam's spirit instinctively discerned the nature and identity of each creature because he was aligned with God's mind. There was no distortion, no interference, no fleshly filter. Adam didn't guess, and God didn't correct him. Heaven endorsed Adam's discernment because Adam was seeing from God's perspective.

The fall reversed that order. Humanity began living from the outside in instead of the inside out. Natural senses took the lead, and spiritual senses went dormant. What used to be instinctive became inaccessible. What used to be normal started being called mystical. The greatest loss of Eden wasn't immortality; it was awareness of God's world.

But God's original intent never changed. That's why redemption isn't just forgiveness—it's restoration. Jesus Christ didn't come only to save us from sin; He came to restore what Adam lost. He came to reopen access, awaken sight, and bring humanity back into revelatory living. When Jesus started His ministry, He didn't just preach morals; He demonstrated a life governed by another realm. Blind eyes opened, deaf ears unstopped, lame legs strengthened, demons fled—not because He was trying to prove power, but because He was functioning from sight.

Jesus said it plainly: He could do nothing on His own, only what He saw the Father doing. That's a staggering statement. Jesus didn't act independently. He didn't heal just because He felt like it—He healed because He saw. His miracles weren't random acts of power; they were expressions of perfect alignment. The Father revealed, and the Son revealed it on earth. That's the pattern for sons. Servants follow instructions, but sons receive insight. Revelation isn't democratic; it's relational.

The devil understands that deeply. He knows that the more revelation someone carries, the more dangerous they become. That's why he pushes counterfeit revelation—knowledge without intimacy, insight without obedience, illumination without alignment. The serpent offered Eve information separated from relationship. God offers revelation that flows from union.

When Jesus trained the twelve, He didn't just teach doctrine; He initiated them into mystery. He spoke in parables publicly but explained everything privately. He trained their spiritual senses. He restored their capacity to see. After the resurrection, the disciples didn't just preach forgiveness—they shook the world. What changed wasn't their passion; it was their access. What Adam lost was being restored.

Carrying God's secrets makes a person dangerous. Revelation produces authority, authority produces impact, and impact threatens darkness. Scripture says it's the glory of God to conceal a matter and the glory of kings to search it out. We're invited into hidden things not to elevate ourselves, but to manifest heaven on earth. The natural mind can't receive these things because revelation is spiritually discerned. Anything untouched by revelation ends up governed by human reasoning, and human reasoning can't build God's Kingdom.

Revelation isn't information, it's unveiling. It's the veil being pulled back. Study matters, but studying alone doesn't produce revelation. Revelation comes when the Spirit unveils truth to the spirit-man. Just like physical senses perceive the natural world, spiritual senses perceive God's realm. Those senses must be trained and matured. In Ephesians 1:18 (NKJV), Paul prayed that the eyes of our understanding would be enlightened, which means eyes exist before they open. Many believers have spiritual sight but never develop it. Revelation needs a foundation. Without grounding in the Word, deeper mysteries can't be sustained. Faith is the foundation revelation rests upon. Without faith, revelation has nowhere to land.

Growth in revelation comes through two main pathways: Scripture and intimacy. Revelation never contradicts the written Word; it deepens our understanding of it. The Word keeps revelation anchored. Intimacy with Christ is the other path because revelation flows from relationship. Peter didn't recognize Jesus as the Christ through logic, but through an unveiling from heaven. In Scripture, knowledge often means intimacy. The closer we are to Jesus, the more we grow in spiritual stature. Glory carries weight. Anointing carries substance. Time in His presence increases our capacity to carry that weight. That's why not all believers function with the same authority. We're equally loved, but not equally entrusted. Authority is given through maturity.

It's possible to be spiritually strong, and it's possible to stay spiritually weak. I've seen how real spiritual authority carries weight in the unseen realm. Revelation often shows up as the inner witness—that deep knowing inside. It's easy to dismiss, but it's foundational. Adam named the animals by instinctive knowing, not step-by-step instruction. His spirit resonated with God's blueprint. That inner knowing isn't imagination; it's alignment. A trained spirit recognizes truth before the mind can explain it.

Before the fall, Adam's spirit was perfectly tuned. After the fall, that clarity was lost. In Christ, it's restored. The believer's journey is the reawakening of spiritual senses—the return to sight. That's why the Kingdom of God isn't just believed; it's perceived. Jesus said unless someone is born again, they can't see the Kingdom. Seeing comes before entering. Revelation comes before manifestation. What you can't see, you can't steward. What you can't perceive, you can't release.

The serpent targeted sight because sight governs dominion. Jesus restores sight because sight releases the Kingdom. The battle between light and darkness isn't mainly about morality; it's about revelation. Darkness is the absence of light. When light shows up, darkness has no defense.

When sons carry secrets, heaven moves through them. When spiritual eyes open, the Kingdom advances. That was God's design from the beginning. That's what Christ restored. And that's the invitation now, to see again. The war over sight didn't end in Eden; it had a change in strategy.

The enemy still fights revelation because revelation governs authority. That's why fear and intimidation are such effective weapons. A fearful church becomes a restrained church. A skeptical church becomes a hesitant church. A church that doubts the supernatural will never contend for its inheritance. Fear closes the door through which revelation comes.

Yes, deception is real. Counterfeit ministry exists. But Scripture never tells us to retreat from the supernatural—it tells us to grow in discernment. Christianity is supernatural at its core. Take away the supernatural, and you're left with religion without power. If the enemy can't corrupt you, he'll try to intimidate you. If he can't counterfeit you, he'll try to silence you. That's how inheritance is forfeited—not through rebellion, but through fear.

A church that refuses the supernatural out of fear doesn't become safe; it becomes powerless. The early Church knew deception existed, yet they still healed the sick, cast out demons, prophesied, and lived aware of heaven's reality. They didn't back away from the spirit realm—they learned to walk in maturity within it. Authority flows through access, which is why the enemy fights revelation so fiercely. Skepticism can sound wise, but often it's fear dressed up as intellect. The natural mind wants control, but the spirit realm isn't navigated by control—it's navigated by revelation.

A church that doesn't see will always be led. A church that sees will advance. The serpent targeted Eve's eyes because whoever shapes perception shapes direction. Today, fear and abuse are used to convince believers it's safer to stay blind. But blindness has never been safe. Jesus didn't restore sight so we could live cautiously; He restored sight so the Kingdom could manifest.

The issue isn't whether the supernatural is real—it is. The issue is whether we'll live in the inheritance Jesus restored. This isn't about chasing power. It's about stewarding what was always meant to be normal. The Kingdom advances through clarity, and clarity comes when our eyes are opened the way God intended.

ACTIVATION

Father, I thank You for giving me the secrets and mysteries of the Kingdom. I ask You to reveal to me the secrets of divine health, provision, healing, deliverance, and every realm of knowledge that will equip me for my purpose. I thank You that I am being flooded with light and perceiving things I could never have known, things that will transform my life and the lives of everyone connected to me and everyone I encounter.

I thank You for exposing the tactics of the enemy and giving me an offensive position in spiritual warfare. I receive divine intelligence that positions me to walk in victory. Give me wisdom to apply this knowledge so that I walk in alignment with Your will and step into everything You have prepared for me.

CHAPTER 9

PARTNERING WITH HEAVEN'S ASSIGNMENT

One of the aspects of unlocking heaven's power is learning to partner with angels. This may sound unusual to some, but Scripture clearly tells us that angels are "*...ministering spirits sent to serve those who will inherit salvation*" (Hebrews 1:14 NIV). As believers in Christ, we are those heirs. Angels assist in carrying out God's purposes. They do not function to serve selfish ambition, nor do they act independently of God's will. They are not moved by human command alone, but by alignment with the heart, mind, and purposes of God. As we partner with the Lord in obedience, prayer, and faith, angels are sent to assist in what He is doing.

Throughout Scripture, we see that different assignments often involve different kinds of angelic activity. Healing, for example, is at times connected to angelic ministry. In John 5, an angel stirred the waters at the pool of Bethesda, and those who stepped in at the appointed time were healed. While our faith remains in God alone, this passage shows that healing can involve angelic participation in God's mercy. When we engage in spiritual warfare, we also see angelic involvement.

In Daniel 10, an angel explains to Daniel that he was delayed by spiritual opposition until Michael, one of the chief princes, came to assist him. This reveals that unseen battles can be connected to angelic conflict and breakthroughs. Likewise, Psalm 35:5–6 speaks of the angel of the Lord pursuing and driving back the enemy, imagery that reflects angelic enforcement of God's justice as His people pray.

Angels are also sent for protection. Psalm 91 declares that God *"will command His angels concerning you, to guard you in all your ways,"* and that *"...in their hands they shall bear you up, lest you dash your foot against a stone"* (Psalm 91:11–12 NIV, NKJV). This language paints a vivid picture of God's protective care expressed through angelic guardianship. Scripture frequently presents angels as messengers bringing divine revelation. An angel appeared to Mary to announce the birth of Jesus (Luke 1:26–38), and angels brought direction to Joseph through dreams, guiding him to protect the Christ Child. These moments show angels participating in the unfolding of God's redemptive plan at crucial turning points in history.

Angels are also shown responding to the Word of God. Psalm 103:20 (NKJV) says angels *"...excel in strength...heeding the voice of His word."* This suggests that as God's Word is spoken and His purposes are declared in alignment with His will, angelic activity can be connected to the fulfillment of what He has spoken. We even see angelic involvement in divine connections. In Genesis 24, Abraham tells his servant that the Lord will send His angel ahead to help him find a wife for Isaac, illustrating that God can use angelic guidance in orchestrating covenant relationships that carry forward His purposes.

Angels also play roles in major redemptive and historical shifts. In Acts 10, an angel appears to Cornelius, telling him that his prayers and generosity have come up as a memorial before God. This encounter leads to Peter preaching in Cornelius's house, where Gentiles receive the Holy Spirit just as Jewish believers did earlier. That moment becomes a turning point in the gospel going to the nations. Scripture also records angels executing God's judgments at times. In Acts 12:23, an angel of the Lord strikes Herod after he accepts worship as a god and does not give glory to the Lord. In Revelation, angels are depicted sounding trumpets, stirring winds, and pouring out bowls that affect events on the earth, showing their involvement in God's end-time judgments and global shifts.

All of this reveals that angels are deeply involved in the purposes and agendas of God—from personal guidance and protection to spiritual warfare, divine connections, gospel expansion, and even historic judgments. They are not the focus of our faith, but they are faithful servants of the God we worship, actively participating in the outworking of His will in the earth. From the beginning of my salvation until now, I have experienced the activity of angels.

My first experience with an angel happened when I was newly born again, and I later shared this encounter on Sid Roth's *It's Supernatural.* One night, as I was asleep, I felt a tap on my shoulder. When I looked, I didn't see anyone there, so I decided to go back to sleep, assuming I was dreaming. Then I felt another tap on my shoulder, but this time it was completely different. I could feel the presence of the glory of God, and it was as if a person was standing next to me, but invisible. At that point, I could no longer deny that I was having an encounter.

The angel began to whisper in my ear, and I could even feel the breath as it spoke. The angel said, "I am an angel of the Lord, and I was sent to bring you a message." At the time,

I wasn't aware that there were different ways God speaks, or that in the Kingdom, there are higher ways of communication than the words we use here on earth. I expected the angel to continue speaking in a way my natural mind could understand, but instead, as the angel began to speak, water poured out of the angel's mouth and went into me. It was the water of life—the water that flows from the Father. It refreshed me, filled me, and opened me up to new levels of sensitivity to the Spirit. It also cleansed and washed me. I was different after that day, and I believe the fruit of this encounter is still evident in my life.

There have also been times when the sound of a trumpet blast has awakened me. When I hear it, I wake up in the night or early in the morning. At first, I didn't always know what to do, but over time, I realized it was a call to pray. Sometimes angels help us stay aligned with what the Holy Spirit is doing, assisting us in prayer when something needs to be intercepted or when God is conveying a special message, and we need help to receive it. Angels also minister to us. The Bible says that when Jesus was in the Garden of Gethsemane, an angel strengthened Him. Many times, when we pray for someone who is far away and in need, angels are sent to minister to them. Sometimes we overlook the fact that we were very depressed one day, and then the next day we wake up feeling much better—it could be that the angel of the Lord was ministering to us.

I began to notice that when I prayed and felt the atmosphere shift or become charged, there was often angelic activity. This was especially true when I was praying in tongues. My prayer language would shift dramatically, and there would be a different spontaneity flowing. On one hand, the Holy Spirit was energizing my prayer, but on the other hand, those

Spirit-filled words seemed to activate angelic assistance. So angels are actively engaged in helping us pray, minister, worship, and even preach. I've discovered that while preaching, angels are always doing what the Holy Spirit is doing. If the Holy Spirit is healing through the laying on of hands, angels get involved as well—especially in an environment of corporate, prophetic, and apostolic worship.

I remember a time when I received a prophetic word from a man of God that there was an angel named Breakthrough who partnered with me in ministry. As I ministered, he would go into the atmosphere and clear demonic disturbances. This was often when miracles, mass healings, and deliverances took place. When I first received that word, I had never actually seen the angel do this, but I could see the fruit. There were times when I wasn't laying hands on anyone, yet as I declared the Word or released strong proclamations, it seemed like everyone in the room began to be touched by God. The angel was helping to bring the breakthrough. I was holding a meeting entitled "Called by Fire." After I finished preaching, I sat on the stage and invited people to come to the altar. As I told them to begin to pray, people all over the room started experiencing deliverance. Diseases began leaving bodies, spirits of infirmity came out, and sexual addictions were broken. Many times, when it seems like everyone is being ministered to collectively, this is the activity of angels.

I have also found that angels are drawn to the secrets and mysteries of God. When we talk about the Kingdom, about Jesus, and about the things of the Spirit, the atmosphere begins to change, and angels go to work. The powerful thing about angels is that they never get tired. They are waiting for us to align with God's will. Our prayers, our decrees, and our prophetic words that express the heart and mind of God engage heavenly activity. It's time to give the angels something to do.

ARCHANGELS

In Scripture, archangels are presented as ruling or chief angels. The term means "leading angel," suggesting rank and responsibility. These angels appear to oversee divisions of the angelic host and carry significant authority in the spirit realm. They are often connected to major movements in God's redemptive plan, spiritual warfare, and the delivery of crucial divine messages. Their assignments are weighty, often involving nations, seasons, and large-scale spiritual battles rather than individual, everyday tasks.

CHERUBIM

Cherubim appear to have the responsibility of guarding holy things, especially the throne and the glory of God. These are not gentle or childlike figures, but powerful beings directly connected to the realm of divine glory. After Adam fell, it was cherubim with flaming swords who blocked the way back to the Garden of Eden, preventing access to the tree of life. This shows their role in guarding what is sacred and restricting unauthorized access to the holy. We also see their imagery woven into Israel's worship. The veil of the temple had cherubim embroidered on it, marking the boundary to the Most Holy Place—the dwelling place of God's manifest presence. Once again, we see that they are associated with guarding the glory. Cherubim seem to work directly to protect God's throne and preserve the holiness of His presence.

SERAPHIM

Seraphim are described in Scripture as "burning ones." They are fiery beings who minister before the throne of God in continual worship. In Isaiah's vision, they cry out, "Holy, holy, holy," declaring the absolute holiness of the Lord. Their ministry is closely connected to purity and cleansing. One of the seraphim took a live coal from the altar and touched Isaiah's lips, symbolizing purification from sin and consecration for service. These angels reflect the cleansing fire of God—the kind of fire that does not destroy His people but refines them and makes them holy when they encounter His presence.

WATCHERS

The Watchers are mentioned in the book of Daniel and are more fully developed in ancient Jewish writings. In Scripture, they appear as heavenly beings who observe the affairs of humanity and carry out divine decrees. In Daniel, a Watcher announces judgment over a king, showing their connection to God's governmental authority. They seem to be linked to oversight—watching the outworking of God's plans on the earth. Some traditions suggest they also record or bear witness to human actions. They represent God's all-seeing nature—His ability to see not only outward actions, but also the heart and motives behind them. In biblical accounts, Watchers are sometimes associated with the execution or announcement of judgment according to God's righteous standards.

ACTIVATION

Right now, in the name of Jesus, I thank You that Your angels hearken to the voice of Your Word. I decree and declare Your divine protection over me, my family, and everyone connected to me. I decree and declare that the angels are lifting me up so that my feet do not dash against a stone.

I decree and declare that, in Jesus' name, angels are scattering every power—resisting me, fighting me, or trying to frustrate my destiny—by the fire of God. I thank You that the angels are assisting in scattering the enemy.

I decree and declare that right now, in Jesus' name, You are releasing ministering spirits to go before me and arrange divine connections, supernatural breakthroughs, miracles, and divine opportunities. I decree and declare that everything stolen from my life is being recovered right now by the fire of the Holy Spirit.

I declare that angels are going forth, assisting me, and securing every part of my inheritance that belongs to me. I thank You for angelic help in everything You have called me to do.

CHAPTER 10

HINDRANCES TO THE POWER OF GOD

The devil fears a man or woman who walks in the power of God. God's world-changing power exposes the devil and pulls the cover off him and his kingdom. When the power of God flows like a river, it is a witness that the gospel is true and that Christ has risen from the dead. The power of God is evidence that satan was conquered and stripped of all authority—his kingdom and all the fallen angels and demons were defeated. He is intimidated by the idea of us believers realizing that he is under our feet because he is under Christ's feet, and we are in Christ. Jesus has disarmed principalities and powers and has been seated high above all the power of the enemy. So this victory of Christ is the basis of why we can enforce the overthrow of satan's kingdom. Just thinking of how defeated he is sends me into a praise!

How can someone who has so decisively and permanently lost appear to be so effective against not only humanity but specifically against Christians? It is because our generation has neglected the message of the cross. We have begun to preach philosophy and, in some cases, have found a way to build churches that do not welcome the Holy Spirit's power and manifest presence. Things change when the power of God is active and surging through us like electricity.

One of the devil's primary hindrances of God's power is persecution. Persecution has different levels. The ultimate being when governments persecute the Church, but there are other ways that the devil manipulates people into rejecting the power of God. He desires not to close the door to churches but to use the Church and make it natural.

This creates a culture where many never see the demonstration of the Spirit's power. Satan strategically wants it to be so normal for there to be no supernatural signs that anything else is strange; the authentic is perceived as strange and cultish. The devil begins to create fear around things that would most tear down his kingdom. This is why he creates so many demonic narratives, doctrines of devils cunning enough to seem correct, but there is no true gospel that divorces us from the power spelled out in the Bible.

The early Church was told in the epistles to pass along and to walk in the faith of those who had gone before them. Our current faith should not be any different from the faith that started in the book of Acts, passed from Jesus to the disciples. This faith manifested in the upper room, spread into Europe, and is even now still moving throughout to the uttermost parts of the Earth.

In God's mind, the Church of today is the same as the early Church—it's one generation. We are living in the same generation as Paul. We are living in the same time period—called the last days—that started on the day of Pentecost. And so, by creating fear around the things of the spirit, satan makes people reject the things of the spirit out of fear of deception. The irony is that you have to be deceived to reject your inheritance, and so many who are trying not to be deceived have fallen into the deception that is created by fear. As a result, they live a powerless life, unable to be world changers in the sense that Jesus was through the gifts of the Spirit.

The devil uses the spirit of offense to hinder the power of God. He wants us to be offended. In Matthew 24, when the Bible describes the end times, and it begins to give all of the signs of the end times, many people focus on wars and rumors of wars, earthquakes, and unusual weather phenomena. They point to all the different things that are going on in the world around us, but one thing is often ignored. He said that many believers will be offended during this time. And one of the spirits of the age *is* offense. The devil has caused people to leave their inheritance because they are offended at the move of God.

John the Baptist experienced something similar, and by looking at the end of his life, we can learn things about offense. He was in prison after confronting King Herod. While in prison, the same John whom the Lord had shown through supernatural witnesses, even with the heavens opening and the voice of God declaring it, that Jesus is the Son of God, was blinded by his offense. We know that he was offended because in Matthew 11:3 (NLV) it says he sent two of his disciples, and he asked, *"Are You the One Who was to come, or should we look for another?"* It was as if he had completely forgotten about what the Lord had done and what happened when he baptized Jesus. And Jesus responded to him, telling him the blind see, the deaf hear, the lame walk, and then He says, *"And blessed is he who is not offended because of Me"* (Matthew 11:6 NKJV).

I believe this speaks to our day as well. The enemy seeks a generation of offended hearts because offended hearts cannot burn with passion. Often, they find themselves embracing things that are not in alignment with scripture, especially if they have been offended by someone who operates in the gifts of the Spirit or emphasizes God's power. As a result, millions of believers today sit outside of God's move due to unforgiveness, bitterness, and offense in their hearts. They have even begun to speak against the move of His Spirit and persecute it because of their offense.

One of the ways that the devil hinders the move of God is through familiarity. The devil aims to raise a generation that is comfortable, lukewarm, and familiar—not only with God, but with His mantles and anointing. This is a unique strategy because whenever familiarity enters our hearts, we cannot receive. Jesus encountered this in His hometown, where He could do no mighty works because of their unbelief. Often, this familiarity is not easily recognized; many may claim, "I'm not familiar with God. I love Jesus." Yet, familiarity may be manifesting toward their pastor, leader, servants, or voices the Lord is using.

This can also tie to offense. We may be offended by whom God chooses to use. We may desire one of our own choosing instead of someone raised up by God. If they do not fit into what we think being qualified looks like, familiarity and dishonor can set in, preventing us from receiving the blessing of their gift. In Galatians, Paul tells the church that they treated him like an angel from heaven or like Christ Himself. I believe this attitude was a key reason why the early Church saw such a demand upon the apostles' lives and experienced explosive, extraordinary events—because power was not blocked by dishonor and familiarity. Honor is not only for leaders; it is something we do because we love Jesus, not just for personal gain. It is also important to recognize that in the supernatural realm, there is a law of exchange. This is why the Bible says if you give a prophet a glass of water, you shall receive a prophet's reward.

Once the devil has recruited people to persecute the Church, the next hindrance is the fear of man inside those who desire to flow in the power of God. Some pastors know that the Holy Spirit moves today or have experienced the power of God, but they are afraid to exercise it because they fear people. The Bible says that if the spirit of glory rests upon you, you shall be hated. Because of the spirit of the age, which is the antichrist spirit, the stronger the glory upon your life, the more you will be hated.

The devil uses this tactic to stop the power of God from flowing by making the vessel so fearful of exercising it that they're afraid to lose their reputation or social status. In the coming days, we will have to choose to obey the presence of God, even over the opinions of men. Paul said we cannot serve Christ while being man-pleasers. Even if it costs us opportunities, we must be willing to flow in the power of God because our generation needs to see it. Our generation needs to know that Jesus Christ rose from the dead, and the evidence is in the message. We must be OK with being misunderstood.

The antichrist spirit is a spirit that opposes anything associated with Christ. It works through the government. It works through relationships. It's anti-anointing. It's against the anointed one. The religious spirit motivates people to tear one another down; therefore, anyone walking with God in the supernatural must understand that he will be misunderstood, rejected, and accused of operating by the wrong spirit. The spirit of the antichrist wants to stop the manifestation of Jesus from flowing out of us. It desires that anyone who's walking in power appear as though he or she is operating under a false spirit.

This happened to our Lord Jesus as He was casting out devils. Some people said He cast out devils by the power of Beelzebub, and some people claimed that He had a demon. If it happened to our Lord Jesus, it can happen to us as well, but this is why the Holy Spirit gives us boldness. This is why the Holy Spirit comes upon us and makes us as bold as a lion. It's time to rebuke the fear of man, the fear of rejection, and know that we would rather be approved by God. The Bible says in Acts 2:22 that Jesus was approved by God through miracles, signs, and wonders. If Christ's approval was connected not only to His character but also to miracles, signs, and wonders, the same is true for us. A sign that we have been sent by God Himself is the power of God. In a day where witchcraft is getting bold, atheists are bold, and many other anti-God movements are bold, the Church cannot afford to be cowardly.

The devil desires a Church full of intellectualism more than one filled with the Spirit. We need doctrine and strong teachings, but it's also important for people to encounter God. Our churches should be places where people come to experience His presence and hear His voice. The prophetic word can awaken someone who doesn't know their purpose. There's something even more profound for someone who doesn't know God, who was rejected by their parents, but is introduced to the loving Father by prophecy. That moment can touch them so deeply that years of pain and trauma can be broken in an instant. The Bible says to know the love of Christ, which surpasses knowledge. Paul was not talking about knowledge that is taught, but knowledge that is experienced. One way God teaches us is through supernatural experiences. This does not replace studying and searching the scriptures, but one encounter with God can give you a lifetime's worth of knowledge.

The sermon cannot turn the atheist; the power of God can do it. I remember years ago, I was preaching, and there was a man who came into my church. He did not believe that Jesus was Lord. He was an atheist. He was a good man. His wife had been radically set on fire by Jesus and had been born again, and she was praying for her husband. She had come to the meeting that day, and her husband had come as well, and it was not the message that I taught that day alone that gave them a miracle, but it was the laying on of hands at the end of the meeting. I started to lay hands on people, and as I was laying hands, people were falling under the power of God, something that in some circles is considered controversial.

Still, when the weight of God comes upon you, it's like when the priest would lay their hand and press all their weight upon the people as a sign of the heavy glory of God. Sometimes God is just waiting so long that you fall, and you can't stand up under it. Well, this man found himself on the floor while being an atheist, and he had a vision of Jesus while he was on the floor; it was not my teaching. It was not my oratory skills. It was not how well articulated the message was. It was an encounter with Jesus Christ. He got up from the floor and gave his life to Jesus. He has been serving Jesus ever since.

A part of satan's strategy is to raise up false ministers who deceive people with false doctrine, drawing them into the counterfeit instead of the authentic, supernatural realm of God. But there is a second layer of deception in this strategy. The devil wants genuine believers to see false teachers operating in the counterfeit by encountering the counterfeit first. His goal is to make them reject the authentic and legitimate power of God that he fears most. The devil wants people to throw the baby out with the bathwater.

Satan also uses the moral failures of genuine men and women of God. When a believer falls, the devil becomes the accuser, and his goal is not only to damage that individual but to shake the faith of the Church. He wants people to assume that because a vessel failed, the message must have been false, too. But the Holy Spirit confirms the Word, not just the person delivering it. That is why it is so important to measure everything by Scripture. If something is truly in the Word of God, a person's failure does not make the truth invalid—it simply means that person went off course.

This is one reason I have purposed in my heart to pray for those who have fallen. My focus is not primarily on whether they return to ministry, but on their restoration in relationship with God. If one day authentic transformation leads them back into ministry, that would be a beautiful testimony of the goodness of God. But even if they never stand in a pulpit again, we can still rejoice that they have been restored to the Lordship of Jesus Christ and will not hear Him say, "*Depart from Me, you worker of iniquity*" (Matthew 7:23, Luke 13:27 adapted).

CONCLUSION

UNLOCKED: LIVING AS A SIGN AND A WONDER

Now you are equipped to be a sign and wonder to your family, friends, and everywhere God sends you. You have been given divine authority to act on God's behalf. You are a portal for heaven to flow through and for the supernatural to be released. Can't you feel the stirring? What is inside you has been unlocked, and you are now ready to flow in the miraculous.

Don't be afraid to take risks. Allow yourself room to grow. Walk in humility and embrace this new journey of walking with God in the supernatural. Your life from now on will be filled with explosive miracles, incredible outcomes, and supernatural breakthroughs. As you step out in faith, you will begin to see that the same Spirit who worked through Jesus is working through you. The impossible will start to bow to the name of Jesus as you speak, pray, and obey His leading.

There is nothing the devil can do to stop God's plan when you remain surrendered and yielded to Him. You are God's voice on the earth. You are God's hands on the earth. You are a carrier of the fire and glory of God on the earth. Heaven's power is inside of you, and because it's in you, it's time to turn the world upside down for Jesus. It's time to become a revival starter in your home, your church, your workplace, and your city.

This isn't about striving; it's about abiding. As you remain connected to Jesus, the flow of heaven naturally moves through your life. Pray for the sick. Speak life into situations where death has taken hold. Release hope where despair exists. Expect God to move when you open your mouth and lay hands on people. You were never created to live a powerless Christian life. You are meant to demonstrate the Kingdom.

So I tell you the same thing Jesus told the disciples in Matthew 10:8 (NKJV): "*Heal the sick, cleanse the lepers, raise the dead, and cast out demons. Freely you have received, freely give.*"

ABOUT CHAZDON STRICKLAND

Chazdon Strickland is a man of many roles—devoted husband to Emily Strickland, nurturing father to five children, and a dedicated partner in their Apostolic ministry based in Jacksonville, Florida. Beyond his family life, he is a prolific writer and the charismatic host of *The Glory Realm*. His life is a testament to his deep commitment to his family and his faith, guiding others through his multifaceted contributions.